PRAISE FOR ~~LESSONS FROM~~

"Dykstra takes a deep dive into Berea's institutional culture and enduring commitment to democratic values. In so doing, she demonstrates how the college's distinct approach to liberal arts education has nurtured generations of low-income and minority students to respect tradition, diversity, and the dignity of work while living a life committed to social justice and civic responsibility. This small college in the foothills of Appalachia has long served as a model for progressive leadership in higher education in America. *Lessons from the Foothills* is indeed a very good read about a remarkable institution."

—Ronald D Eller, author of *Uneven Ground:*
Appalachia since 1945

"Dykstra captures the significant and unique role of Berea College in American higher education. Since the nineteenth century, more than any other institution, this college has been a national model of excellence in educating low-income students. For years, Berea was known to be the higher education institution in the South that had the moral courage to openly promote integration between the races. Students get to know each other, come to appreciate the dignity of work, and study the liberal arts as they prepare to lead and serve in the larger society. The reader will be amazed by the inspiring stories of the Berea educators, students, and alumni who continue to have a substantial impact on Appalachia and beyond. Berea has been a college whose vision was far more than a century ahead of its time."

—Freeman A. Hrabowski III, president emeritus,
University of Maryland, Baltimore County

"From its initial impetus to create a collegiate environment dedicated to racial coeducation to its focus today on equality and environmental sustainability, Berea College has long been a force for positive change in the Appalachian region. Gretchen Dykstra has written a significant and appreciative study of how Berea College has excelled in realizing the values to which it is committed. Admirers of Berea College and

readers interested more generally in the impact of higher education in Appalachia must not miss the opportunity to read this important book."
—Dwight B. Billings, University of Kentucky professor emeritus of sociology and former president of the Appalachian Studies Association

"With the keen eye of a gifted storyteller, Gretchen Dykstra weaves a rich tapestry that sheds light on a question asked by every admirer of Berea College: How does this small institution, nestled deep in Appalachia, outpace virtually every other American college on every metric that matters? The story of Berea, beautifully documented in this engaging book, reflects Berea's deep commitments to racial equality, community empowerment, and the transformative potential of education. The remarkable success of the Berea idea is more than simply inspirational. The Berea story also poses a radical challenge to the country's educational establishment: work harder to open wide the door to opportunity."
—Jeremy Travis, president emeritus, John Jay College of Criminal Justice

"Berea College has been disrupting the norms of higher education ever since its inception as an interracial school in a slave state before the start of the Civil War. Gretchen Dykstra offers a history of this small liberal arts college in the Appalachian foothills. Just as important, she artfully describes how the college is continuing to build on its commitment to 'impartial love' to address the needs of the current student body."
—Tim Marema, Berea College graduate and editor of *The Daily Yonder*

"There is a small but venerable college nestled in the Appalachians, where students are offered a rich curriculum taught by excellent teachers. No tuition is charged, though the students are expected to help with the upkeep. The average annual income of the students' families is $27,000. Half the students are white and half are Black or Latino. Most of them are the first in their families to go beyond high school. This against-all-odds institution is Berea College, and Gretchen Dykstra does a masterful job of telling its story."
—Conn Nugent, chairman emeritus, the Land Institute

LESSONS
FROM THE
FOOTHILLS

LESSONS
FROM THE
FOOTHILLS

BEREA COLLEGE AND ITS
UNIQUE ROLE IN AMERICA

GRETCHEN DYKSTRA

Gretchen Dykstra

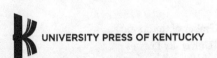

UNIVERSITY PRESS OF KENTUCKY

Published by the University Press of Kentucky,
scholarly publisher for the Commonwealth, serving Bellarmine University,
Berea College, Centre College of Kentucky, Eastern Kentucky University, The
Filson Historical Society, Georgetown College, Kentucky Historical Society,
Kentucky State University, Morehead State University, Murray State University,
Northern Kentucky University, Spalding University, Transylvania University,
University of Kentucky, University of Louisville, University of Pikeville, and
Western Kentucky University.

Editorial and Sales Offices: The University Press of Kentucky
663 South Limestone Street, Lexington, Kentucky 40508-4008
www.kentuckypress.com

Cataloging-in-Publication data is available from the Library of Congress.

ISBN 978-1-9859-0068-4 (hardcover : alk. paper)
ISBN 978-1-9859-0069-1 (pbk. : alk. paper)
ISBN 978-1-9859-0071-4 (epub)
ISBN 978-1-9859-0070-7 (pdf)

This book is printed on acid-free paper meeting
the requirements of the American National Standard
for Permanence in Paper for Printed Library Materials.

Manufactured in the United States of America.

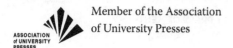

Member of the Association
of University Presses

ASSOCIATION
of UNIVERSITY
PRESSES

To the students of Berea, past, present, and future

CONTENTS

THE GREAT COMMITMENTS

First, to provide an educational opportunity for students of all races, primarily from Appalachia, who have great promise and limited economic resources.

Second, to offer a high-quality liberal arts education that engages students as they pursue their personal, academic, and professional goals.

Third, to stimulate understanding of the Christian faith and its many expressions and to emphasize the Christian ethic and the motive of service to others.

Fourth, to promote learning and serving in community through the student Labor Program, honoring the dignity and utility of all work, mental and manual, and taking pride in work well done.

Fifth, to assert the kinship of all people and to provide inter-racial education with a particular emphasis on racial healing and equity among Blacks and whites as a foundational gateway toward understanding and equality among all peoples of the earth.

Sixth, to create a democratic learning community dedicated to gender equality.

Seventh, to maintain a residential campus that encourages in all community members a way of life characterized by mindful and sustainable living, health and wellness, zest for learning, high personal standards, and a concern for the welfare of others.

Eight, to engage Appalachian communities, families, and students in partnership for mutual learning, growth, and service.

INTRODUCTION

I spotted a one-inch-by-one-inch advertisement in the *Atlantic* that said, "Visit Appalachia with Berea College." My grandmother had told me years before about Berea College. I did not remember the details, but I remembered her enthusiasm. I signed up. It was June 2011.

We were a disparate group of 24 from Dallas donors to Vermont environmentalists, Louisville lawyers and New York lefties, and me. We started with two days of lectures at the college before driving in a bus throughout eastern Kentucky, southern Virginia, and into Tennessee. We saw the horrifying and the beautiful; we met mining activists, union members, frontier nurses, community doctors, cultural leaders, ministers, and political organizers. We saw mountains whose tops had been blown off with dynamite, and we attended a Pentecostal church service where women and men sat separately and snakes were coiled in wooden cages. We visited Appalshop, where radio, film, and music capture past traditions and create new ones, and we had lunch in a Black church in an abandoned mining town where many congregants have returned in their retirements.

On the last afternoon of our four-day tour, we bumped into ten tattooed, middle-aged, leather-clad white motorcyclists in the parking lot at the Comfort Inn in Kodak, Tennessee, heading toward the Cumberland Gap. They were gearing up to roar off.

"Where y'all from?" one motorcyclist called as we climbed from the bus.

"Berea College," someone answered, and in unison, the cyclists cheered and gave a collective thumbs-up as they thundered off.

I began returning to Berea over the course of many years, with time out during the COVID-19 pandemic and writing another book. I have met scores of students, some serendipitously, some arranged. I have attended classes and lectures and had long conversations with professors and administrators. I have interviewed alumni, both recent and not so recent. I have corresponded with some who know the college, and I have sat in local cafés, the cafeteria, and the hotel lobby to eavesdrop on conversations. I have driven throughout eastern Kentucky, meeting some of the college's Appalachian partners, and I have pored over archives in the Hutchins Library for hours. It has been endlessly interesting and, at times, inspiring, and it all started on that tour and the motorcyclists' cheer. May I do this special institution justice.

1

BEREA TODAY

Founded in 1855, the private, four-year, coeducational liberal arts college on a hilltop in central Kentucky was the first interracial and coeducational college in the South. Today, Berea educates about 1,600 academically talented students, chosen for what its Admissions Office calls "grit and fit." Every year 75 percent of those students come from the poorest counties in Kentucky and Appalachia.[1] Another 18 percent come from around the rest of the States, and 7 percent are from 70-plus nations.[2] About 45 percent of the student body are young people of color. Rooted in nonsectarian Christianity, it is not a Bible school, although as many as 40 percent of the students might come from evangelical Christian homes. They live and learn with Muslims, Buddhists, Hindus, and atheists.

What garners Berea the most attention, however, is that *every* student receives free tuition for all four years; *every* student works in service to the college community to cover most of the other costs, and *every* student comes from a family living under the poverty line. In 2023, 96 percent of Berea students were Pell eligible (or would be if they had citizenship), and the average family income was $27,000. Fifty percent of the students graduate with no debt, and those who do averaged $2,078 in 2022–2023.

Although national ratings of colleges are often exercises in public relations, the *Washington Monthly* magazine's annual assessment, which uses three criteria, in 2023 rated Berea second among all four-year liberal arts colleges in the nation.[3] That same year, the *Wall Street Journal* listed Berea and Stanford as the two best colleges for their value.

Recognition of Berea tells an interesting story. I am not a professor; however, my world in New York consists of highly educated people, and I often meet new people. In the years since I have been working on this book, I have met only one professor who had not heard of Berea. The college is a member of many relevant associations, from the Appalachian College Association to the National Association of Independent Colleges and Universities and the Work College Consortium; its 138 professors, each with an annual budget for conferences and symposia, attend and present at annual meetings, and many publish articles and books in their respective fields. But as President Emeritus Lyle Roelofs, a physicist, once said to me, "If someone wants to be a big player in his or her field, Berea is probably not the right place. We respect scholarship, but teaching is our top priority." Yet even in my unscientific survey, scholars know about this little college in the South.

Michael Crow, the innovative president of Arizona State University, calls Berea "an aspirational, regional prototype." Scott Cowen, president emeritus of Tulane University and author of *Winnebagos on Wednesdays*, writes about visionary leaders and strong missions and cites Berea and how its remarkable history still shapes its current values.

Some professors appear envious of its clear mission, almost competitive with its achievements. Citing Berea, I asked one such professor, responsible for sustainability at his elite institution, how his college embeds environmental stewardship into student life. He flicked his wrist at me and said dismissively, "Oh, that's Berea," and yet in *every* sustainability measure, Berea surpasses his institution. In fact, the Association for the Advancement of Sustainability in Higher Education in 2019 ranked Berea number one among some three hundred colleges for its promotion of sustainability.

Scholars and researchers from all over the world visit Berea's Hutchins Library to use its extensive special collections and archives. Many civil rights activists know Berea well—Congressman John Lewis was a huge fan—and Berea's participation in actions, like the historic March on Selma, is legendary. Its list of speakers is a veritable who's who of social justice movements.

American folklorists and folk artists know about Berea and its role in preserving the cultural richness of Appalachia. Berea's sound archives are nationally and even internationally known, complemented by an extensive music program, with most students participating in some musical activity, such as the integrated Black Music Ensemble and the Berea Bluegrass Ensemble. The annual Berea Crafts Festival attracts hundreds of artists from the entire region, and the town of Berea has been named the craft capital of Kentucky. The college's own Student Craft program, initially begun to provide income to women artisans in the hollows, provides labor assignments to students and reaps wide respect, not for turning out professional artists (although there are some of those), but for keeping the folk crafts alive and spreading their beauty elsewhere. The sustainably managed Berea forest has trails called the best in the state, and its five hundred-acre organic farm is the longest continually run college farm in the nation.

So why, others ask, do so few "regular" people know about Berea? The answer is, of course, what people, where? In central and southern Appalachia many people know about it, but elsewhere the answer is not so much. I've been talking about Berea for several years now, and I'd guess that only one out of ten people have heard of it. For a long time, Appalachia has been reduced to stereotypes of isolated and dysfunctional families that the mainstream press and films perpetuate by highlighting mining disasters, crippling unemployment, and opioid addiction.

Students arrive at Berea, often the first in their family to go to college and with no influential or wealthy family connections, no elaborate social and professional networks, and no easy entrée with media elites. There are no moneyed legacies at Berea, no mighty links to economic leaders or social influencers. One particular news article underscored how Berea is ignored. It was about alumnus Nathan Hall ('10), who worked as a coal miner before enrolling at Berea. He majored in agriculture and natural resources before getting two graduate degrees at Yale. Then, he returned to central Appalachia to farm hemp on degraded mountaintops. Hall told Berea, "I have the same mission now that I had when I started Berea in 2006: to help transition the coalfields into a sustainable environmental future." The article never cited Berea, only Yale.

Given Berea's regional focus, college counselors outside the region, even if they know about Berea, usually do not offer it as an option to their students, as only about 350 students come from outside Appalachia. Most of the non-Appalachian students or alumni with whom I spoke found the college online.

And lastly, Berea, as an institution, emphasizes community service, not the accumulation of wealth, status, or power. It's proud of its illustrious alumni, including a famous historian, a Nobel Prize winner in chemistry, a former secretary of labor, a plaintiff in the US Supreme Court case that gave everyone the right to marry, and a deeply religious, well-known doctor and former provider of abortions, but the college is equally proud of those who do good and important work back in their local communities. It's not a lack of imagination or ambition—or even opportunity. Almost 50 percent of the students have at least one international experience during their time at Berea, many have paid internships over the summers, and all are exposed to a wide world on campus. But with little or no debt upon graduation, an emphasis on service, and a deeply engrained love of community, many Bereans return home as teachers, nurses, environmental activists, and artists while others go to graduate school or into tech and financial fields. It's the ethos of Berea. President William Hutchins (1920–1939) described ideal graduates as "ordinary people doing extraordinary things in service to others."

How can the college afford to do what it does? Berea stopped charging tuition in 1892, even though at that time, Elizabeth S. Peck writes, it had just $100,000 in its endowment. With that promise of free tuition, every administration has recognized the imperative to raise funds, and in 1920, the board decided that all unrestricted bequests would build the endowment. That last decision has never been changed. In June 2021, Berea ended its fiscal year with more than $1.5 billion in its endowment—about the ninety-fifth largest in the United States.[4]

But, most significantly, Berea spends the interest from that endowment *only* on students, covering approximately 74 percent of the cost to educate them. Berea combines those funds with federal and state grants and annual private contributions to close the gap. The student bodies of other private four-year liberal arts colleges, even those that declare a commitment to equal opportunity and have large endowments, average 15 percent low-income students. It's the will, not just the money, that distinguishes Berea.

The first donors were primarily northern abolitionists and then people interested in helping a southern state after the Civil War, and particularly a state that had many Union supporters. Over time, the number of donors has numbered in the thousands and today includes friends, alumni and their children and grandchildren, private foundations, trusts, and more than 450 students, who donate $1–$10 monthly from their own labor wages. Interestingly, many individual donors to Berea do so in addition to supporting their own colleges or universities, recognizing the unique and enduring mission of Berea. One recent alumnus put it straight. "It has a good product to sell."

Additionally, Berea, as a work college, has lower operating costs than other colleges. Although it costs money to manage the Labor Program and supervise the students in it, students provide more than 160,000 hours of much-needed labor to run the institution annually. The fully residential campus is well equipped and green, but it has none of the expensive amenities that some colleges need to attract tuition-paying students or satisfy wealthy donors. There are no dormitory suites with private bathrooms, no rock climbing walls or international squash courts.

Some people ask why the college focuses exclusively on economically marginalized students. They argue that middle-class and upper-middle-class students could pay their own way and open future professional doors for their less well-heeled classmates.

"Keeping rich kids out is as important as keeping the poor kids in," Nancy Gift, the Kentucky-raised and Harvard-educated Compton Professor of Sustainability, said. "I can discuss food stamp policy in my ag classes, and everyone has a story, and no one feels ashamed." No students are marginalized at Berea for their poverty. Brian Reed ('99), who has been a senior administrator at several colleges and universities, including Dartmouth and Vanderbilt, puts it slightly differently: "At colleges with both low-income and middle-class kids, I have watched as every student's debt increases with all the talk of clothes, restaurants, and spring breaks. Berea does not tempt students with those distractions."

How does Berea stay Berea? How does it stay true to its ideals, and how does it continue to innovate as its founders did? Berea is not carved in stone; it has, over time, adapted to new opportunities and changing realities, and it has stopped doing things that did not work or were no longer useful. Its most severe external test came in 1904 when Kentucky passed the Day Law, aimed solely at Berea, which prohibited integrated colleges in the state. After losing its appeal at the US Supreme Court, for forty-six years Berea was unable to address its founder's fundamental aspiration for equal educational opportunity for Blacks and whites.

In addition to that historic struggle, Berea has had its own internal debates about priorities and approaches: One president,

William Frost (1892–1920), reduced Black enrollment to match the percentage of Black people in the state and actively sought students from the mountains. In its early days, Berea had an elementary school, a high school, and a normal school as well as a college; it did not become just a college until the tenure of William Hutchins. Much to its lasting chagrin, the college refused to host the training for the Freedom Summer in 1964, and in 1970 not everyone on campus wanted the college to drop mandatory chapel; some push for greater disinvestment from oil and gas, and some faculty complain about salaries, others about the workloads. A staff member quit in reaction to the introduction in the Student Craft of a rainbow baby blanket, and in 2020, a professor's felony arrest for distributing child pornography and his subsequent suicide rocked the campus.

Like at most colleges, and particularly at an interracial, gay-friendly college in a conservative southern state, there are town and gown issues. In 1968, a gunfight in the town of Berea resulted in the deaths of a local Ku Klux Klan member and a Black protester. More recently, there have been ugly incidents of racial and homophobic epithets hurled at students as they walk down the street that bifurcates the campus. Derrick Singleton, Vice President for Facilities and Sustainability, acknowledges that Berea College is a proverbial blue dot in a red state. But then it always has been.

Berea's racial, gender, political, and religious diversity can cause tension among students, and the college readily admits that strains exist, but building community—Berea's fundamental approach—is never easy, and the college leans into such problems with an intentionality that encourages discussion and disavows avoidance. It treats tension as part of the educational experience.

I first experienced that around 2013 when I returned to Berea for the first time after the 2011 tour. The External Affairs Office asked a male student to pick me up at the Lexington airport in a college car. A tall, red-haired junior with a cheerful demeanor, he was raised in Gays Creek, Kentucky, which he described as a "little spot on the road" at the base of a mountaintop removal site in eastern Kentucky. He lived in the house his great-grandparents built that "was big in love, if not in space." His father, a former coal miner, was an addict with no access to mental health services, and his mother was a part-time postmistress. "We are a strong family unit, deeply rooted in school and church," he told me. Majoring in Appalachian studies, he hoped to do community development work when he graduated and meanwhile was learning about civic and political life by advocating for gay rights.

Several days later, a young sophomore woman took me back to the airport. An evangelical Christian from northern Georgia, she had wanted to go to Oral Roberts University but came to Berea because of the free tuition. I asked her if she knew my earlier driver; she didn't. Then I asked her thoughts about gay rights. She paused and then answered, "Love the sinner, hate the sin."

I dropped it, but I told someone in the Communications Office about the exchange, not to tattle but as an example of my growing awareness of differences at the college. Several months later, when I next returned to campus, someone in the Communications Office had arranged for me to have dinner with the two of them so that we all could get to know one another. We had a pleasant evening, talking about their classes, their work assignments, and life at Berea. There was laughter and ease, and that's the intentionality of Berea.

So how does the school maintain this historic commitment to what its founder, John Fee, called "impartial love," and how does a college institutionalize enlightened practices so that they outlast their innovators? Michael Crow, again, responds, "An innovator has to create a culture that embraces aspirational values . . . and then translate that to mission, goals and design." Berea has built such a culture, and the Great Commitments guide it.

During the 1960s, the antiwar movement challenged people's view of American interests and responsibilities, and advocates for women's liberation, Black power, and environmental action demanded recognition and opportunity. Berea's president Francis Hutchins took the values that represented what Berea held dear, summarized them for a proposal, and later President Weatherford and the board formally accepted them. Tweaked occasionally, those Great Commitments define the college and its values and provide a shared narrative for the entire community as well as the structure for this book.

When Chris Lakes ('99), director of the Office of Student Success, was studying for his doctorate in educational leadership, one of his professors asked his graduate students to read aloud the mission statements from their respective undergraduate institutions.

"When he reached me, the professor said, 'Wait.' My heart sank, and I thought 'Oh, no, he doesn't think I belong here,'" said Lakes. "But, no, after everyone else had finished, the professor, who was the retired president of Louisiana State University, returned to me and said, 'Now listen to this one. Berea is the only college in America that has a mission statement that actually guides the college.'"

You could summarize the mission of the college with "learn, serve and work," but those words only communicate what students do, not who they are and how the college helps them flourish. The Great Commitments as stand-alone goals do not communicate their interconnectedness, but taken together, they provide a clear roadmap to building what Martin Luther King Jr. called "the beloved community." Berea is dedicated to building a community of unlikely allies with curious and discerning people ready and able to make the world a better place.

"It's hard work, and we are not there yet," as several Bereans have said to me, but these commitments serve as Berea's North Star.

2

JOHN FEE, HIS COURAGE, AND HIS CLARITY

"Bundle up your books and come home. I have spent the last dollar I mean to spend on you in a free state," an angry Kentucky father wrote to his son. It was 1844, and John Gregg Fee was a divinity student at Lane Theological Seminary in Cincinnati, Ohio, led by the dynamic and controversial Dr. Lyman Beecher.[1]

Young Fee had arrived at Lane two years before, after having studied at Miami University of Ohio and graduating from Augusta College. He had grown up on his family's tobacco and hemp farm, where they enslaved thirteen people and traded others.

"I was often scolded for being so much with the slaves and threatened with punishment when I would intercede for them," Fee later wrote in his autobiography. Despite that affinity, he had never questioned the bondage of human beings until two friends at Lane challenged him. "These brethren became deeply interested in me as a native of Kentucky and . . . my relation to the slave system. . . . They pressed upon my conscience the text, 'Thou shalt love the Lord thy God with all thy heart, and thy neighbor as thy self,' and as a practical manifestation of this, 'Do unto men as ye would they should do unto you,'" Fee wrote.

When he received that blistering letter from his father, young Fee, already an ordained Presbyterian minister, returned to Kentucky intent on fighting for the immediate abolition of slavery. He initially lived with his parents, trying in vain to convert his father, a stubborn and strict man, who, as Fee also wrote, never "opened the door of his heart to the sentiments of freedom for the slave."

HIS LOVING WIFE AND COMRADE

Young Fee knew he would face a life, as he wrote, of "obliquity, perse-cution and peril." But he found a loving partner in Matilda Hamilton, also from northern Kentucky, whom he had known from their rural church in Bracken County, southeast of Cincinnati. A light-hearted and friendly young woman, Matilda came to her courageous com-mitment naturally. Her mother, a Quaker, once hid an enslaved fugitive in the family's basement when a bounty hunter came to the house looking for him. Fee knew that story and the impact it had on Matilda's abolitionist sympathies, but when Matilda underwent a fully immersive baptism—an act that signified the continuum of life and death and the acceptance of Jesus Christ's resurrection—Fee knew they shared something else profoundly important.

They married in 1844. She was twenty, and he was twenty-eight.[2] Fee later wrote that Matilda gave him "affection, sympathy, cour-age, cheer, activity, frugality and endurance, which few could have combined, and which greatly sustained me in the dark and trying hours that attended most of our pathway." That path led through rural Kentucky.

SLAVERY IN A CHRISTIAN STATE

With its temperate climate, grasslands, and tree-covered mountains, Kentucky was not a "plantation state" if measured by the size of the farms, but it was a slave state. In 1840 when Fee left for Lane Theo-logical Seminary, Kentucky had about 800,000 people, including 225,000 people enslaved by 32,000 white people. The farms were concentrated in the northeast and central parts of the state, where tobacco, corn, and hemp grew and where slave owners also leased their enslaved laborers to local farmers and shopkeepers or sold the Black children or elders to plantations farther south.

Whether they owned enslaved people or not and whether they could read or not, most white Kentuckians used the Bible to justify slavery. They would cite Abraham, whose household included enslaved people; the Ten Commandments, which never condemned the practice; and Jesus, who remained silent on the subject. But young Fee would hear none of it. Christianity represented an entire belief system, not isolated stories. With encyclopedic knowledge of the Bible, he argued forcefully against those interpretations, relying on the creation myth, gospel stories, and Jesus's own use of the golden rule as God's ultimate charge: "You shall love your neighbor as yourself." For him, Christianity was solely about the moral power of its values, not contradictory stories.

Fee became an itinerant preacher, riding through the countryside with a saddlebag full of pamphlets and his Bible, from which he cut out references to slavery, and preaching against slavery.[3] Often physically harassed, Fee was once pelted by rocks thrown by gun-toting men who dragged him from a gathering, and Matilda, fearless and angry, rode her horse between her unarmed husband and his tormentors, challenging them to hurt a woman.

Sometimes only three people came out to hear him, rarely more than fifteen. To preach that slaveholding was unchristian took courage, and to listen did too. Fee would pass a hat, making a pittance. Several times he was offered a church if he would stop talking about slavery, but he always turned them down, unwilling to stop his advocacy.

"I will not sell my convictions . . . to that which I regard as an iniquity, nor my liberty to utter these convictions for a mess of pottage," he wrote in his autobiography.

Elizabeth Embree Rogers, the wife of his future colleague at Berea and a teacher herself, described Fee in her diary as "sandy complexioned, kindly in heart . . . with the sterner stuff of which he was made ever back of his general laugh and kindly voice."

JULETT'S PAIN

John and Matilda sold some land in Indiana that Fee's father had given him many years before, but rather than easing their own poverty, they used the money to buy freedom for Julett, an enslaved house laborer on Fee's parents' farm. Appreciative but ambivalent, Julett did not want to leave her children and grandchildren, and so, even though free, she stayed on the Fee land. Later, however, when she learned that some of her children and grandchildren would be sold, she "kidnapped" two sons, three daughters, and four of her grandchildren and fled. Fee's father had her tracked down, arrested, and jailed, and from her cell Julett watched as slave traders separated and then sold the children. Kentucky might not have been a plantation state, but it was a brutal state.

COLPORTEURS AND FREE BIBLES

The American Missionary Association (AMA), founded in upstate New York in 1846, raised money—mostly in the North—to support abolitionist churches and ministers in the North. But soon the AMA realized that supporting free churches in the South was potentially more powerful than supporting abolitionist churches in the North. In 1848, it began to support John Fee and his work. Historian Stanley Harrold estimates that there were fifteen abolitionist missionaries in the entire South between 1848 and 1861, many inspired by Fee's movement to deny slaveholders cover in churches.

The AMA also supported the printing and distribution of Bibles and abolitionist pamphlets, some written by Fee himself, that laid out the Christian argument for abolition. The state of Kentucky never forbade the teaching of reading and writing to enslaved people. Although the literacy rate was high among white people as well, the fact that some Black people could read was threatening to anti-abolitionists. Men known as colporteurs distributed the pamphlets free to whoever would take them.

Colporteurs were usually northern abolitionists, but Fee insisted also on hiring local men who knew the countryside, the people, and the dangers. The task was part time, arduous, and poorly paid—usually twenty dollars for twenty-six days—and Fee often found colporteurs unreliable and often prejudiced. Robert Jones was the exception.

Born in 1810, Jones lived in Clover Bottom Creek in hilly Jackson County with his wife and thirteen children. An abolitionist and a Methodist, the semiliterate Jones spent a month learning the job alongside Fee and suffering the same indignities, including an attack by two men who stripped Jones naked, whipped him with sycamore switches, and threatened to dump him into a river before galloping away. But nothing deterred Jones, who, although "abused, threatened, beaten, tarred, humiliated and underappreciated, plod[ed] on through the mountains, undeterred, book bag around [his] neck, stubborn, tough and resilient," wrote Fee.

CASSIUS CLAY AND JOHN FEE

The preaching and the pamphlets brought Fee notoriety and stature in addition to introducing Cassius Marcellus Clay into his life. Clay became Fee's patron, giving him ten acres of land that would grow into Berea. The third son of a hugely wealthy Kentucky landowner and slaveholder, Clay, square of build and round of face, was a savvy and colorful man, politically ambitious, and pugilistic as well as an abolitionist who freed his own enslaved laborers as proof of his intentions.[4]

His support for abolition was economic, not moral. He believed that a diversified economy could take root in Kentucky as it did in New England, and he blamed slaveholders for impeding change.

Although Clay supported the gradual abolition of slavery, not immediacy, he admired Fee and became his benefactor—for a while.

In the mid-1850s, Clay purchased six hundred acres of land in central Kentucky and offered Fee ten acres if Fee would live there and minister to the community. The Fees accepted and, with three horse-drawn wagons, moved more than one hundred miles south to an overgrown ridge that looked east to the Appalachians and west to the rolling hills of the bluegrass region. The new settlement became Berea, named for a town in the New Testament where Jews and Christians lived together harmoniously.

CLAY AND FEE REDUX

In 1855—six years *before* the start of the Civil War—Fee opened a one-room school inside the small wooden church that he had built in Berea. The school would enroll anybody eager to learn, Black or white, at any level. He described its purpose "to educate not merely in a knowledge of the sciences . . . but also in the principles of love in religion, and liberty and justice in government; and thus permeate the minds of the youth with these sentiments."

The arrival of a few Black students initially drove some white students away and, although they returned, someone, horrified by the very thought of Black and whites, boys and girls, men and women, learning together, burned down the school. Fee rebuilt it and someone burned it down again. Berea professor Jason Strange writes, "The school in some ways was more incendiary than preaching anti-slavery."

On the sultry afternoon of July 4, 1856, a few miles outside Berea at Slate Lick Springs, hundreds of people gathered to picnic and hear speeches about the upcoming presidential election. Cassius Clay and John Fee were both there and got into a vitriolic debate over slavery.

Fee argued, as always, that slavery was a moral issue—saying a higher law dictated what was right or wrong, not man-made laws. Therefore, he continued, the Fugitive Slave Law, passed six years before, which compelled *all* citizens, Northern and Southern, to return enslaved runaways to their enslavers and paid federal agents to hunt them down, was itself illegal. These words were fighting words for the aggressive Clay. As an elected official himself, Clay argued vehemently that slavery could be changed only politically. Then with characteristic bombast, he declared Fee a "revolutionary, insurrectionary and dangerous."

No matter what their reaction to the debate might have been, everyone there took note of Clay's harmful retreat from Fee. "His known opposition to us was a power more potent and depressing than all the mobs of the state," Fee later wrote.

Without Clay's tacit protection, Fee faced more threats and more physical danger; he was once dragged from a house to witness the brutal beating of a colleague. "These were dark days—days in which we could walk only by faith, not by sight," he wrote in his autobiography.

THE LITTLE SCHOOL GROWS

In 1858, invited by Fee, Reverend John A. R. Rogers, a graduate of Oberlin, and his wife, Elizabeth Embree Rogers (a teacher too), came to Berea to teach in the little school. "The underbrush was so dense," wrote John Rogers, "a rabbit had to pin his ears back to get through it."

By that spring more than one hundred students from seven to twenty-nine years old were studying, off and on, in the one-room schoolhouse, and in June a curious Cassius Clay, whom Fee had not seen since their disagreement two years before, came to the school's first commencement.

"Fee, things look better than I thought they would," Clay said. "I am at heart as much a 'higher law' man as you are, and if we were in Massachusetts, we could carry it out, but here we cannot."

"Moral truth should not be confined to geographical limits," Fee replied.

Not persuaded on the validity of the school, Clay refused to serve on its newly formed board of directors. It was one thing to oppose slavery; it was something entirely different to educate Black people with white people, particularly white women with Black men. Abolition of slavery did not mean equality between the races. Indeed, opposing slavery did not translate into respect for Black people, and some of Clay's writings were blatantly racist. "They [Black people] lack self-reliance. We can make nothing out of them. God has made them for sun and bananas."

Clay might have refused to become a trustee, but a few other local men served on the board and together purchased about one hundred acres of land on the ridge, sending Fee north to raise money. It was the autumn of 1859.

MISINFORMATION TRAVELS FAST

Henry Ward Beecher, the minister at the famous Plymouth Congregational Church in Brooklyn, New York, was the quintessential fiery abolitionist preacher. Son of Lyman Beecher of Lane Theological Seminary, flamboyant Henry believed that the Union had to be destroyed if slavery was not. In crates marked "Bibles and Books," he sent rifles to the antislavery activists in Kansas; the rifles became known as Beecher Bibles. His infamy grew and he was detested in the South. Hearing that Fee was coming to New York in the late fall of 1859, Beecher invited him to speak, hoping to shine on Fee what historian Christi M. Smith calls "the abolitionist limelight."

On October 16, 1859, John Brown and a small group of Black and white men attacked the weapon arsenal in Harper's Ferry, Virginia, hoping to arm an enslaved uprising. The raid failed and Brown was hanged within six weeks. Newspaper headlines around the country blasted the news of John Brown's audacity, fueling the growing fear of Southerners' worst nightmare—Black people slaughtering white people.

John Fee rejected such violence and said at Beecher's church soon after the raid, "We want more John Browns; not in manner of action, but in spirit of consecration; not to go with carnal weapons, but with spiritual men who, with Bibles in their hands, and tears in their eyes, will beseech men to be reconciled to God. Give us such men and we may yet save the South."

The Lexington and Richmond newspapers picked up the story of Fee's sermon, misquoted him, and published false accusations, saying that Fee was hiding a cache of weapons. Fee's neighbors in Madison County and beyond now saw the little rural town of Berea and its one-room integrated schoolhouse as a locus of potential violence. An estimated 750 angry white men converged on the county seat to vent their fear and fury and chose sixty-five prominent white men to demand the Bereans leave.

EXILED

On Christmas Eve 1859, the angry emissaries arrived in the town of Berea, a place already harassed by others. Elizabeth Rogers wrote about that December night, "I thought I had known danger before. I had lain awake nights trembling at every noise. I had stood terror-stricken before drunken crowds, who used to swagger up and down our streets, but here was a more savage element than ever before."

Thirty-six members of the Berea community fled, including Matilda and three of her children, who headed north in cold rain and snow across the Ohio River to the free state of Ohio and the city of Cincinnati. The Fee's youngest son, three-year-old Tappan, died from the exposure on that journey. John Fee met them in Cincinnati.

FEE AT CAMP NELSON

When the Civil War began in 1861, fearful of a Northern invasion, Kentucky remained neutral, but both Union and Confederate armies moved into the state to recruit soldiers. Armed militias, loyal to one side or the other, skirmished and raided railroads and supply depots around the state. Kentucky became pockmarked with ragtag factions of angry and violent men.

In June 1864, President Abraham Lincoln declared that any enslaved person, including enslaved men from Kentucky, could win their freedom by enlisting in the Union army. Men, such as Gabriel Burdett, a freedman who had enlisted in the Union army at Camp Nelson, south of Lexington, spread the word, secretly and dangerously, among the enslaved men of Kentucky. It was said a farmer could go to sleep with thirty enslaved laborers and wake up in the morning to discover he had none. Within two months approximately fourteen thousand enslaved men—approximately three-fifths with the scars of whippings—escaped and made their way to Camp Nelson.[5] Soon their wives (or those considered wives, since at the time enslaved people could not legally marry) and children followed—some after having been beaten in retaliation for their men's disappearance. John Fee and his son, Burritt, were there, too.

"I know you, all about you, and have for years and will give you every facility I can," said Quartermaster Theron Hall, who had heard Fee preach in Massachusetts. "But we want teaching for these colored men as well as preaching. They . . . need to be taught to write [and] sign their names to their reports."

"Furnish me a house and desks, and I will secure teachers and do the work," Fee responded.

Fee got the space. Soon almost seven hundred men and eight women were attending the Camp Nelson School for Colored Soldiers. Fee preached at night and taught during the day along with eight teachers and materials sent by the AMA. One of the teachers was eighteen-year-old E. Belle Mitchell. The daughter of two freed people who had bought their freedom before her birth, Belle had spent time in Xenia, Ohio, where she studied to become a teacher. Impressed with her and eager for an integrated teaching staff, Fee, who had met Belle at a Black church in Danville, Kentucky, convinced her parents—perhaps somewhat naively—to allow her to join him back at Camp Nelson. But when Fee and Mitchell arrived at Camp Nelson, most of the AMA teachers refused to eat with Belle. It was all right for Belle to teach Black soldiers but not to eat with white teachers. Racial prejudice runs deep, even among the well-intentioned.

"I will suffer my right arm torn from my body before I remove the young woman," Fee responded angrily; however, the protests against Belle continued, and when Fee left the camp briefly, the superintendent told her to leave. She moved to Lexington. Her future brother-in-law would eventually become the first Black graduate of Berea College.

TERRIBLE PAIN AFTER THE WAR

At the end of the Civil War, without their own land, many former enslaved people moved into towns—by 1868, there were more Black people in Lexington than white people. But jobs for them were few and wages low, if paid at all. If a Black worker complained about not being paid, he'd risk being "blacklisted," or blocked from other jobs. Police routinely arrested unemployed Black men for vagrancy and sent them to jails, where they were "leased out" as farmworkers. Freed people desperately needed and wanted schooling, and some began simple, church-based schools, but the schools were often burned, their poorly prepared teachers harassed, and their students intimidated.

The federal government established the Bureau of Refugees, Freedmen, and Abandoned Lands to ease the transition from slavery to freedom, but the agency left Kentucky within a few years, with one administrator writing, "Mobs utilized mock lynchings, beatings, house wrecking or burning, rape, emasculation and murder in their efforts to establish social, economic and political relationships, based on white supremacy."

But Fee did not leave Kentucky. Leaving Gabriel Burdett and Fee's oldest son, Howard, to run the school at Camp Nelson, Fee returned to Berea in late 1864, encouraging several dozen Black people whom he met at Camp Nelson to join him.

BEREA'S NEXT CHAPTER

John Fee and John Rogers reopened the school with no money and no structures on 109 acres of woodland. "The object of this 'college' will be to furnish the facilities for a thorough education to all persons of good moral character, at the least possible expense to the same, with all the inducements and facilities for manual labor which can be reasonably supplied," Fee wrote.

Nearby communities vehemently opposed the school. The students had to ignore the rigid societal expectations of them, dictated by both race and gender: white students had to overcome their racial prejudices, Black students had to endure that prejudice, and white women were expected to interact with Black men. But soon both Black and white, men and women, with dramatically different educational levels, studied, worked, and ate together. John Rogers wrote, "We had cheerful courage amid poverty and opposition."

John Fee in the woods. Courtesy of John G. Fee Papers, Berea
College Special Collections and Archives, Berea, Kentucky.

By 1867, the Berea Literary Institute had ninety-one white
students and ninety-six Black students, including fourteen of the
fifteen children of Henry and Elzira Ballard, a Black couple who
had come from Camp Nelson. With an official charter, a survey,
and stipends from the AMA for nine staff members, Berea began
to grow.[6]

By 1868, the AMA had a representative on the board who served with Fee, Rogers, several local men, and Gabriel Burdett from the Camp Nelson school. The students included Belle Mitchell, the young Black woman who was forced to leave her teaching post at Camp Nelson; she enrolled at Berea in 1868, and there met her future husband, Jordan Jackson.[7] The Freedmen's Bureau supported scholarships as well as the funds needed to build Howard Hall. Named for the one-armed Union general Oliver O. Howard, chairman of the Freedmen's Bureau and founder and president of Howard University, the three-story, white clapboard dormitory housed eighty-nine men. Razed in 1971, its tin-roofed tower with a weathervane was saved and today marks the Howard Hall Memorial Park on campus. The school had an interdenominational chapel, makeshift classrooms with partitions for flexibility, several small frame houses for boys' and girls' residences, a $10,000 endowment, and, in 1869, its first president, E. Henry Fairchild (1869–1889).

THE FIRST GRADUATES

Fifty-four when he arrived at Berea, E. Henry Fairchild had been an active abolitionist and then, as an Oberlin alumnus, led its preparatory school. He arrived at Berea with similar values to those promoted at Oberlin and the professional experience to direct a school where more than two-thirds of the students studied at the elementary and secondary levels. In the spring of his first year, President Fairchild enrolled the first college class.

In 1873, three white men became the first graduates of the college; the following year, two white men and two Black men graduated, including the brother-in-law of Belle Mitchell Jackson. Then in 1875 two white women and one Black man graduated. In a report to the board, an unnamed author described the graduation this way: "When we look upon the crowd of two thousand people, colored and white, rich, and poor, learned, and ignorant, mingling without distinction and with prefect order, listening to speakers and singers of all shades of complexion, the words on the college seal seem wonderfully appropriate: 'God hath made of one blood all nations of men.' Twenty miles from this line, on either side, such a company could not be gathered."

THE DEATH OF JOHN FEE

John Fee died suddenly at home on January 11, 1901, at age eighty-four. Reverend James Bond, an early graduate of Berea and the future grandfather of the distinguished civil rights leader Julian Bond, eulogized Fee, saying, "He loved men, not conditions; humanity,

John Fee's funeral procession. Courtesy of John G. Fee Papers, Berea College Special Collections and Archives, Berea, Kentucky.

not races or nationalities. . . . John G. Fee was a benefactor of the world. His name and deeds are the heritage of humanity." Judge W. C. Taylor wrote in the *Lexington Herald-Leader*, "His life and work of love was as broad as human existence."

Fee was buried in the Berea cemetery. When he died, Berea had educated more than 1,700 students in four different academies. It had trained scores of Black teachers and administrators, who staffed the growing number of schools for Black people, including presidents of Kentucky State University, the first Black land grant college in the state. It had a printshop, a woodworking shop, and a brick shop, and it had purchased more land. Luckily, Fee never experienced the tragic impact of the Day Law.

JIM CROW HIJACKS BEREA

Sometime in 1902, a state legislator, Carl Day, visited Berea, saw an interracial couple hugging, and was appalled. He moved quickly to force a change. Using as its basis the notorious 1896 *Plessy v. Ferguson* decision by the Supreme Court that allowed segregation, the Kentucky state legislature passed the Day Law in 1904 and forced Berea to segregate immediately or pay a fine of $1,000 a day.[8]

Berea's President William Frost (1892–1920) had already begun to divert Fee's enlightened experiment in racial equity. When Frost first arrived at Berea, there were 182 Black students and 172 white students, but soon he argued that the racial ratio on campus should mirror the state's racial ratio, which hovered around 7:1, white to Black. Furthermore, Frost had traveled into the mountains of eastern Kentucky and, in 1899, published a widely heralded article in the *Atlantic* describing the poor white people he met as "our contemporary ancestors." He actively began to champion that population, changing the admission policies and raising money with stories and handicrafts from the isolated mountain people. It was, perhaps, powerful to remind northerners that Appalachians from Kentucky were not slaveholders and many supported the Union during the Civil War. On the eve of the Day Law, there were 962 students at Berea, and 805 were white.

Although Frost lobbied to defeat the proposed Day Law and even solicited legal help from a well-known Boston lawyer, the college—and Fee's aspirations—faced fierce opposition by the state legislators and local businesspeople. The Kentucky superintendent of education said, "Berea is a stench in the nostrils of true Kentuckians."

After the passage of the law, aimed solely at Berea, the trustees announced it would support any Black Berean who transferred to an all-Black institution, and fifty-two students transferred to Fisk, Hampton, and Tuskegee. That act magnified the belief among some that Frost had secretly masterminded the elimination of Black students. Frost pushed back on those accusations, even writing defensive statements in New York newspapers.

The college also sued, lost the appeal at the Kentucky Court of Appeals, and, with $30,000 (about $1 million in current dollars) from Andrew Carnegie to support the legal work, appealed to the US Supreme Court to hear its case. In 1908, Berea lost again when the Court decided that a state could force a private institution to segregate. Ironically, the lone dissenter was John Marshall Harlan of Danville, Kentucky. That loss garnered national attention and, as historian Eric Foner writes in an email to the author, "further legitimatized Jim Crow."

The school took steps to design and build a new campus for Black students. Dedicating $200,000 (almost $7.5 million in current dollars) from its endowment, the school solicited another $200,000 from Andrew Carnegie, $50,000 from an anonymous donor, and $20,000 from four thousand Black Americans in gifts from $0.50 to $200. It hired Vertner Woodson Tandy, a young Black architect from New York, and landscape architect Frederick Law Olmsted Jr. to design the Lincoln Institute on a hill outside Louisville. It opened in 1912 with eighty-five Black students, primarily to be trained as teachers; its main administrative building was named Berea Hall.

But the lovely new campus did not mitigate the pain, the arguments, the hurt, or the anger that the community of Berea endured internally, including questions of why it was Black students who had to leave.[9] Although the college regularly invited Black speakers, musicians, and alumni to campus and hosted interracial conferences for students, it was hardly the same as learning, working, and serving together. John Fee's radical aspiration was stopped.

In 1950, the Day Law was finally rescinded—forty-nine years after John Fee died—and Berea slowly began, not without problems and challenges along the way, to reintegrate.[10] In 2021, some 45 percent of Bereans identify as Black or Latino, reinvigorating Fee's vision of the "Berea experiment in impartial love."

On campus, I occasionally heard faint rumblings about whether Latino students fit into Fee's original vision of Black and white students learning together, but such statements were always posed more as questions, not tensions. Likewise, when I asked people which commitment they liked the best, the Fifth, with its emphasis on "equality among Blacks and whites," and the Eighth, with its emphasis on Appalachia, came up most frequently. One alumna said simply, "I hope the college always aims for fifty-fifty, Appalachian whites and Appalachian Blacks."

Berea's origin story and the Day Law are well known on campus. The history is taught and the founders' courage celebrated. Providing a shared narrative helps inspire and galvanize students to overcome the obstacles they all face and keep alive Fee's desire for impartial love.

3

EDUCATIONAL OPPORTUNITY

To provide an educational opportunity for students of all races, primarily from Appalachia, who have great promise and limited economic resources.

"We thought it was a scam," Eve Gettelfinger ('23) told me when her family first learned that Berea was tuition-free. "What's the catch?" she said. No catch. Berea has been tuition-free since 1892.

Eve, a short, talkative brunette, is one of twelve children, brought up by her parents on an eighteen-acre subsistence farm in Lawrenceburg, Kentucky. Only ninety miles away, Berea was too close to home for Eve, but the free tuition and Labor Program were strong draws and won the day. With a double major in theater and psychology, Eve hopes to work with veterans suffering from PTSD. "Many people seem scared to work with them, but I'm not," she said with assurance. "I am also interested in special events, so next year I will study in France and learn about wines and weddings."

With a service orientation, exposure to a wider world, and no debt, Eve can discover new opportunities, explore options, and let her imagination take her to new places. About twenty colleges in America offer free tuition for all their students, but Berea is the only one that *only* enrolls low-income students with high academic potential. In 2020, the average Berea family income was $27,000, and the median American household income was $67,521, according to the US Census Bureau.

WHO ARE THE STUDENTS?

About 70 percent of the approximately 1,600 students come from Appalachia, primarily but not exclusively from the racially and ethnically diverse counties of eastern Kentucky, West Virginia, and northeastern Tennessee, some of the most impoverished areas in the United States. Another 18 to 20 percent (approximately 350 students) come from the rest of the United States, and the final 5 to 7 percent (120 students) are international students, representing seventy-plus different countries. No college of its size in America is as diverse—racially, ethnically, culturally, and geographically. In 2021–2022, 43 percent were Black or Latino, not counting the international students. Fifty-seven percent were first-generation college students.

They live together on the campus with its classic redbrick buildings—some constructed with bricks made by students or with wood harvested by them. Banners of alumni hang from light poles around the campus, prominent signs list the Great Commitments, and yard signs identify trees or remind passersby that some weeds are good for ecosystems.

John Fee's initial one-room church and school, long since replaced, were on the same ridge looking east to the knobs that mark the start of the Appalachians and west past rolling hills to the flat bluegrasses of horse country. Berea's Boone Tavern Hotel, with its four two-story columns, sits on the Old Dixie Highway at a four-way crossroads that is the virtual center of the college, the college farm with its fields and livestock wraps around the ridge, within easy walking distance from campus, and the 9,500-acre Berea Forest with its Forestry Outreach Center is a bike ride away and stretches far to the east.

HOW DOES BEREA FIND THE STUDENTS?

"We look for success before we look for the sob story," said Luke Hodson ('02), Associate Vice President of Admissions, whose sunny office is in an old, pleasantly renovated white clapboard house with a welcoming front porch at the periphery of the campus. "We are a college, first and foremost, not a charity. The art comes in spotting who has the will to break the cycle of poverty and the desire to give back. Those are key traits for a Berean."

Berea is known for its high academic standards, its labor requirements, and its service orientation, so "Berea busy" is a common lament among students. "It's really hard," said Tyler Boggs ('23) from Whitesburg, Kentucky. "Many of my high school classmates were too scared to even apply."

In 2021–2022, the acceptance rate was 33 percent. That compares to the rate of better-known colleges, such as Howard, Vassar, Bryn Mawr, or Spelman, and shines a spotlight on the Admissions Office. How does it recruit such potentially strong (often) first-generation college students from low-income families; who does it accept; and how does it support them once they arrive?

A tall, lanky former basketball player, Hodson, one of four children, grew up in Knott County, a former coal mining hub in eastern Kentucky. When he was born, some 76 percent of the county residents lived under the poverty line. Hodson was one.

His parents were local missionaries who engrained in their children a commitment to service. Hodson volunteered with church groups and at youth camps throughout his childhood and graduated third in his high school class. He knows now that he checked important boxes for admission, but he only focused on Berea when the grandfather of a former schoolmate suggested Hodson send a "highlight tape" of his basketball prowess to the college. "I never knew such a thing could help with college, but my parents and I pulled one together and sent it off, and I began to hear from the assistant coach at Berea," Hodson said. "Then we visited."

Although Hudson's parents were college educated, most low-income students, particularly first-generation kids, are less likely to have ever visited college campuses or have attended summer preparatory programs; they lack any exposure to higher education and often receive no encouragement to attend college, so their aspirations are often sadly limited. If they do think about college, they have little help with choosing one that suits their temperament and interests, and they certainly do not have high-priced college advisers or test prep tutorials to help them navigate the world of higher education. Berea applicants are *never* on the screens of college fundraising offices, and it gives no legacy advantage.

Berea has some distinct advantages in its recruitment efforts, which serve it well as many colleges now actively seek a more economically and racially diverse student body. Its regional focus means it can concentrate its recruitment. Additionally, its historic commitment to students from low-income families and racial equality, even if once perverted by the Day Law, means that Berea did not become woke yesterday. DEI (diversity, equity, and inclusion), an unknown term in 1855, encompasses the college's foundational values, and it has worked hard to achieve Fee's original vision.

Even private colleges with much larger endowments than Berea's rarely have enrollments of more than 15 percent low-income students. Amherst College is a notable exception offering needs-based financial aid and with students of color making up 60 percent of its student body; it ranks number ten in the *Washington Monthly* assessment, with 21 percent being Pell-eligible. But many colleges with large endowments enroll just one or two such students each year. In fact, the *Journal of Blacks in Higher Education* reported in October 2021 that despite impressive increases in endowments, the percentage of Pell-eligible students *decreased* from 2019 to 2021 at nine of the ten private colleges with the largest endowments. Not at Berea. Berea sets aside an application if the student is not from a low-income household. A brochure puts it succinctly, "The Best Education Money Cannot Buy."

GRIT AND FIT

Berea has seven full-time admission counselors, all but two of whom graduated from Berea. In addition to them, four recent Berea graduates are hired for two years after their own graduation as part of a post-graduate program called Berea Corps. The staff is divided by region, with two permanent counselors living in Birmingham and Louisville, where Berea has long relationships with area high schools and where these counselors actively recruit many strong Black, Latino, and white students. The admissions counselors visit high schools, make connections with community-based organizations and religious leaders, and encourage nominations from alumni and others. But they are more than just salespeople—they, too, are mission-driven.

Alicia Riley ('12), an admissions counselor, grew up in Lewis County, Kentucky, where her mother worked in a shoe factory and her father, who had a seventh-grade education, was a tobacco farmer before becoming disabled. In high school, she was ineligible to take the two Advanced Placement courses offered, so she took honors classes when she could, earned several business certificates from the local vocational school, worked about twenty hours a week at the local newspaper, and participated in the school's marching band. Her high school bus driver, whose son was a freshman at Berea, first told her about the college, and every time their paths crossed, the bus driver urged her to apply.

At Berea, Alicia majored in elementary education, and then, graduating debt-free, she went on for her master's in counseling at Morehead State University before landing a job at Gear Up. Gear Up, a federal program, focuses on college readiness, working with local partners in economically disadvantaged areas throughout the country to introduce sixth and seventh graders to the idea, expectations, and value of a college education and how to identify a good college for themselves. Riley flourished at Gear Up, working for five years throughout eastern Kentucky and West Virginia, and then she returned to Berea. "I wanted to give back to the college that gave me so much," she said.

Riley now shepherds from seventy to eighty students through the application process. "I call, I email, I text them or their parents, sometimes as often as ten times. Our stories are an important part of who we are, but how we overcome those challenges are just as important," Riley said. "The educational journey often looks different for every student, and we look for people who have already shown determination. That's the grit."

Katie Roach ('22) grew up in Oak Ridge, Tennessee. Late one Saturday afternoon, she and her mother went directly from Katie's soccer game to her high school college fair. "We looked at all the colleges there and talked for a long time with the guy from Berea. He invited us to join him and other students for more talk in a classroom after the fair closed. My mom got all excited. I wasn't paying much attention. But then the guy showed up at my father's funeral later that week and I was amazed," Katie said. "That said a lot about the college." It also said a lot about Katie. There she was, the week her father died, playing soccer with her team and attending a college fair. A candidate of great promise, for sure.

Riley and her colleagues also listen for a commitment to community. "Everyone here has poverty in common, but we want them to feel comfortable beyond that. We look for the kid who despite a crazy family, terrible economic conditions, or really rigid cultural expectations already has shown a concern for others," Riley said.

Rachel Hidding ('21), a natural resources and agriculture major, grew up in Indianapolis with her two siblings and her widowed mother. "My mother used to take us every afternoon to see my father for an hour in the nursing home. Every Sunday, we took him to church and then Arby's for lunch," Hidding said over Thai noodles at a local restaurant owned by a Berea graduate. "He died of Parkinson's disease when I was nine."

But undeterred by grief, she became an active environmentalist by the time she was twelve, writing a book and producing a video for younger children about climate change as well as winning a scholarship to France one summer.

"That's the fit," explained Riley. "We are recruiting for the entire campus, not just a class."

Many private, four-year colleges seek the grandchildren, children, siblings, and even cousins of alumni—the legacies—hoping the "fit" will be generational, maintaining connections with the college and enhancing fundraising goals. Berea does not accept legacies.

Sometimes the "fit" might be in sports, as it was, in part, for Hodson. Many colleges give scholarships to athletic students—sometimes even if they do not need financial help—wanting to have strong teams to build school pride and maybe future fundraising muscle. Berea appreciates how sports engender enthusiasm and community, but it does not give athletic scholarships—it does not need to—and sometimes students come invested in sports, first and foremost.

In Hodson's first-year class there were fifteen would-be male basketball players; only three stayed with the game and only four graduated—a far worse graduation rate than the rest of his class. "Some of those guys were smarter than me, but that's where the crystal ball of admissions gets fuzzy," Hodson said. "They had enough grit to succeed, but if I were to guess, I'd say they didn't put academics and labor and sports in the proper order."

GENDER RATIOS

In 2019 (before COVID-19 impacted lives and disrupted trends), some 5,200 students applied to Berea; 1,966 applications were completed and considered, and Berea accepted 595 students—30 percent of the pool. Of those accepted, 60 percent identified as women.[1] That ratio worries Hodson. "I'll be disappointed if we stay at 60–40, women to men, but pleased if it doesn't drop further," he said. In 2021, the ratio was 59 percent to 41 percent.[2]

The imbalance between men and women is challenging at many colleges nationwide and, perhaps, even greater when dealing with low-income students. If higher education is not part of a family's tradition and all income, however limited, is needed for the entire family, staying home with a part-time job, joining a trade, or getting a certificate from a community college can be an attractive alternative to four years of a liberal arts education, even if that education is affordable; the family still loses the income, and it represents a four-year hiatus before the student can make a steady income.

In May 2022, the *Chronicle of Higher Education* published a special supplement devoted to this gender discrepancy, offering other reasons, too. Traditionally, boys have lower academic achievement in high school and more nonacademic diversions than girls. In weak schools, this academic discrepancy only gets worse between girls and boys as they age and intellectual insecurities mount. Some suggest—although many dispute—that the more girls achieve and women advance, the more boys and men retreat. Berea has a particular problem attracting white Appalachian men.

"The start of hunting season," explained Vice President for Alumni, Communications, and Philanthropy Chad Berry, "is the saddest day for white men at Berea."[3] Berea does not allow hunting in its forest or guns on campus.

Hodson and his colleagues believe that COVID-19 and vaccination resistance in Appalachia made things more difficult. Berea was the first college in the state to close in 2020, and then, when it reopened, it established strict protocols. They wonder, too, if Berea's embrace of diversity—minorities and gay people, specifically—deters white male students, exacerbated by political divisions and enflamed rhetoric.

Josh Noah ('08), a gay alumnus from North Carolina with a PhD in cultural anthropology, suggests that maybe the nation has reached its peak with college-educated people and wonders if it might be a generational change. Noah cites his brother, who trained as a plumber and "made good money" before he died. "Personally, I see this shift as a positive thing as it encourages more entrepreneurship, which is the ultimate freedom in my opinion," Noah said.

Growing distrust of educational institutions and their priorities play a role, too, in the drop in male enrollment. Specifically, resistance to liberal arts has deepened, and specialization in most fields only exacerbates this. A broad education, too often, is seen as irrelevant and elitist, particularly if it does not immediately flow into a job and help pay off student debt. Every time I met a studio art, philosophy, or English major at Berea, I was reminded of the freedom to explore one's passions when a college education is free.

THE HARSH REALITY OF FINANCIAL REALITY

Tuition is only a piece of the financial puzzle of college. Berea might waive tuition for all its students, and does so in large part because of its endowment, but the other costs, like housing, books, and food, add up quickly.[4] Retaining first-generation students from low-income families between the first and second year is a perennial challenge for most colleges. With little, if any, experience estimating total college costs beyond tuition, most Pell recipients in the United States discover quickly that they will incur debt to fill the gap and drop out accordingly.

The National Student Clearinghouse Research Center tracks the percentage of Pell-eligible students who return to college after their first year, a key factor in predicting educational attainment. In 2021, its data showed that 71 percent made the transition; at Berea, 88 percent did. Clear messages about cost implications are crucial to achieving this.

Berea provides a Family Engagement Counselor to prospective students on all aspects of the financial aid maze, including the application for Pell grants, better known as FAFSA (Free Application for

A student arrives on campus. Courtesy of student photographer Christopher Rice/Berea College.

Federal Student Aid). With FAFSA, the US Department of Education determines how much a family can contribute to the total cost of college (expected family contribution), based on the family and student's income, size of household, and the age of the oldest parent. If a family's income is $27,000 or less, the student will receive the maximum Pell amount, $6,495 (in 2021), with no expectation of any family contribution. At Berea, whatever the difference is between a student's Pell grant and the total cost of room and board is covered through a combination of the students' labor earnings, private donations, some scholarships, and loans. More than half of Berea's 1,600 students graduate with *no* debt; the debt for the other half equals as little as $500. (If students incur more debt, it is usually because they take advantage of Berea's numerous international study opportunities, a percentage of which sometimes must be paid for by the student.)

One week after acceptance, the prospective Berean receives a reminder about the no-tuition promise as well as a preliminary estimate of the total annual cost, even before all sources of potential aid have been finalized. Once calculated, Berea sends another letter—in the same font, color, design, and language of the initial acceptance letter—to all successful applicants with the exact amount that they will pay in Year One. There are no unwanted surprises for the prospective student.[5]

THE YIELD

Not all accepted students enroll. The percentage is known as the yield. The students sometimes choose another college, usually a local community college; some prospective students, particularly Black students, prefer cities, which are more diverse and familiar to them than the tiny town of Berea. Some experience a pressing family issue that requires their staying home or, in some cases, the family cannot afford to lose the kid's wages, no matter how minimal. In 2019, 74 percent of accepted students enrolled, but in 2021 that number was down to 59 percent. The Office of Institutional Research and Assessment believes that drop is related to COVID-19 and to the increase in funding for students at community colleges.

Sometimes parents are the obstacle. "Usually it's the deeply religious ones, who worry that their kid might lose his faith or are uncomfortable with such diversity. If we can convince those reluctant parents that their child will not change, but rather be challenged, we are usually home free," said Hodson.

LaTia Owens ('21) was not sure she wanted to go to Berea, but it wasn't her mother's resistance. A young woman with a one hundred-watt smile from Chicago, she was among the 18 to 20 percent of Bereans accepted from outside Appalachia. The second daughter of a single mother who works as an assistant to a nurse in a Chicago public school, LaTia graduated from the city's highly selective high school for the performing arts before applying to Berea and Jackson State University, a historically Black college in Mississippi. Of her decision to attend Berea, she said, "I thought I wanted big-school things like a marching band and football games. But I came to Berea because of the free tuition, and I'm really glad I did. Beyond the free tuition, the Labor Program has been great. I have worked in the Office of Student Life. I've been a resident adviser in a dorm. I've managed the theater's box office, and now I'm working in admissions. I will graduate in theater and African American studies without a dime of debt. Oh, I also had a paid internship at the Fort Lauderdale Film Festival."

OPPORTUNITY WITH SUPPORT

Financial aid is not enough for the long-term success of low-income students. Many low-income students often come from weak high schools and need a mix of supports, including writing help, remedial math, mentors, academic advisers, and support groups. The former director of admissions at Berea, now at Grinnell College, Joseph Bagnoli, said pointedly, "Opportunity without support is not access."

But few American colleges offer such an array of services—they are expensive, for starters. Yes, Berea has a large endowment—$1.5

billion in 2021—but the difference in the provision of supports rests with both the ability to pay for them and the will to provide them. The interest from Berea's endowment pays for most of the tuition costs, including faculty salaries, which are competitive but not huge. The college raises approximately $3,000 per student per year to fill tuition shortfalls and provide necessary supports. That's the will.

The personal attention begins for first-year students in the summer with information sessions online and a week of orientation. Forty first-year students, who win a raffle, come to campus a full month before for mini-Berea.

"I lived in a dorm, took two classes that met five days a week, and worked," explained Suneil Avirneni ('24) from southern Oklahoma. "I took a course on cults and communes in frontier America, which was really interesting. We read a lot, wrote a lot, and even got to visit a Shaker community in Ohio. People once thought Shakers were a cult. I took a virology course where we studied the coronavirus, and I was a facilities assistant. That's really a janitor."

During the regular orientation week for the other first-year students, the college celebrates Move-In Day with upper classmates helping, and then four full days of tours, explanations, meetings, and registrations. By the end of week one, every Berea student has an academic adviser, a labor supervisor, a student adviser, and a student chaplain in their dormitories.

STUDENT COUNSELING

Students who need writing help can get it from students selected to provide it. Almost half of the students take remedial math, and students who need or want emotional counseling can get it, too, through affinity groups, student chaplains, or professional psychologists.

"COVID, Black Lives Matter, anti-Asian hate crimes, Trump's insults, DACA, Afghanistan, and now the Russian invasion of Ukraine have driven a dramatic increase for our counseling services," said Channell Barbour ('91), the former vice president of Student Life. The day after Barbour told me this, I attended a class on the foundations of peace and social justice and met such a student. Professor Jason Strange was teaching the class. He writes on the college website, "I fell in love with reading as a child, which led to many wonderful things, not least of which was dropping out of high school . . . and spending much of the next decade in the unwalled classroom of the world."

That day he was drawing out of his students the structures of capitalism, based on their own experiences: ownership, labor, markets, costs, benefits, regulations. I walked out of class with a young woman who had described the horrific conditions of jade miners back in her home country.

"I found your comments illuminating and heartbreaking," I told her. "But I'm afraid I do not know which country you meant."

"Myanmar," she answered.

"Oh," I responded, aware of its bloody civil war. "I'm sorry. That's a troubled nation now, isn't it?"

"My mother lives near all the danger, and I have not spoken to her for many months. I'm worried, and I have trouble focusing, but counseling helps," she offered without embarrassment or shame.

Samson Kitenda ('23) from Uganda by way of Cincinnati, who majored in political science with a minor in law and ethics, said, "I gained more than I ever thought imaginable . . . I got funding for LSAT prep and the test, free dental work. I studied abroad. I got a clothing stipend, internships, and real concern for me from professors."

BRIDGES OUT

The college also offers supports to help "students cross the bridge to a larger world—one [that] many of them have never encountered," Vice President Berry said. For instance, the Center for Internships and Career Development helps students find summer internships, including seven tiers of possible financial support. In 2022, one biology student, for instance, landed an unpaid internship at New York University to research opioids; Berea's Center for Internships granted him $7,500 to cover all his travel and living expenses plus a stipend.

Most dramatic, perhaps, of all the bridges out are the many chances for international travel. Half of all Bereans (domestic students only) spend a term abroad or join international study trips. A lucky few travel with musical groups. For young people, some of whom have never been outside their county, let alone their country, these can be life-changing experiences.

Ashley Long Seals ('08), from a tiny town in Southwest Virginia, had never been on a plane before she went to Egypt one January on what Berea calls a short semester. I asked her why she wanted to go. "My daddy would love to travel, but he has never had many chances, so I went when I had the chance," she explained. "I felt privileged. The Lord has been good to me."

"What was the best part?" I asked.

"One Friday we visited a Muslim family in Cairo. They had gone to the mosque, the mother was in the kitchen, and the whole family was there—aunts and uncles and cousins—just like my Sundays in Virginia."

The Egyptian father knew Seals was the lead singer in the Bluegrass Ensemble and asked her to sing.

"I am a Christian and I sing about Jesus, and I don't want to offend anyone," she said to him. "You won't offend us, he said, so I sang in their living room just as I would at home. They liked it, and I appreciated my sweet mama's voice even more."

Berea pays for 75 percent of a trip abroad if it's related to the student's major and 10 percent in a minor field. Some endowed funds support other trips, such as service learning; sometimes students will borrow money to go, and sometimes the students win competitions. In 2020, three Berea seniors won prestigious Watson

Fellowships, each receiving $36,000 to support their worldwide travels as they studied plastic waste, goats, and yoga. In the summer of 2022, student groups explored the Holocaust in Germany and the cultures of Ghana, and twenty-one Berea students won coveted, fully paid Gilman Scholarships, administered by the US Department of State.

BUBBLE OR MICROCOSM?

Some people wonder—faculty, staff, and even some students—if Berea is a bubble, overly protective, nurturing an unrealistic view of the world, and isolated from difficulties, or if, on the other hand, it is a microcosm, showing the students the "real" world with its myriad expectations, harsh realities, and opportunities. In my decidedly unscientific survey, the overwhelming majority of the students I met who believed Berea was a "bubble" were international students, who, by definition, have already experienced more of the world.

Whether a bubble or a microcosm, Berea administrators know that to flourish in an unknown world takes confidence. Alumni often mentioned that when kids from low-income households experience a new world, a more cosmopolitan world, a world with those who have the privilege of broad experiences, the imposter syndrome is a real challenge and sometimes detrimental to future success.

"I had never interacted with rich people," said Cassie Chambers Armstrong, author of *Hill Women: Finding Family and a Way Forward in the Appalachian Mountains,* in an interview at Berea. She grew up in Kentucky, went to Harvard and then Yale Law School, and now serves on the Berea Board.

"I spent a lot of time at college on Google trying to decode society. What was the significance of those little gold hearts on thin gold chains that every girl seemed to wear?" she said. "I constantly tried to hide and redefine myself, pretending my experiences with horses was the same as theirs."

Berea cannot take away all those feelings, but it can lessen some of the mysteries that highlight the differences. Every several months, for instance, the Office of Student Success and Transition hosts a dinner for fifty to sixty students at the college's event space at the Boone Tavern Hotel. "Tonight, we are going to enjoy a formal dinner with informal conversation as we explain dining etiquette," said a young staff member, dressed in a suit and heels, standing in the front of the room. The young guests sat at round tables of eight, covered with white linen tablecloths and set with multiple utensils and glasses.

The staff member continued, "Mastering these simple rules make professionals more professional and will help you in the future feel comfortable, chatting and networking, and not worrying about the table setting and others' expectations. First, please remember no cell phones or elbows ever on the table. Men, you will probably wear a jacket. It's best to keep it on unless your host removes his. Remember the napkin will always be on the left. Pick it up when you sit down, but please don't shake it out like this." She demonstrated and everyone laughed. "Open it and lay it neatly across your lap." They watched attentively and followed carefully.

Student waiters then served a four-course meal as the hostess gave relevant lessons between the courses: tricks to remember which side the bread and the water go on,[6] which fork to use with which course, how to hold your knife, how to cut meat, when you can use your fingers, when you shouldn't. She told a story about President Lyle Roelofs, who cut a tomato the wrong way and squirted his hostess in the face with the juice. Everyone laughed again.

I sat in the back, surprised by an apparent lack of cynicism—no one rolled their eyes, no one whispered, everyone seemed focused. I remembered Professor Gift, whom I had met on an earlier visit, saying, "No student at Berea feels ashamed of their poverty."

The next evening, I met three students for supper whose labor assignments were in the Center for International Education. LaDarious (Samez) Lawson ('24), a biology major from Talladega, Alabama, had been at the supper the night before, and I wondered if he had been bored or, worse, insulted. "I wish I hadn't left my church clothes at home," he said when I asked how he liked it, and then he added, chuckling, "I sure wish I was from Europe so I wouldn't have to worry about switching my fork and knife all the time." Then he added. "I loved the dinner."

"I wish we could go to more than one," added one of his companions.

BREAKING THE CYCLE OF POVERTY

Berea tries to ease transitions, provide necessary supports, and build close connections between students, mentors, and faculty, but one-third of the students who begin do not finish. That statistic stays depressingly consistent with the National Center for Education Statistics reporting that in 2020 the six-year graduation rate for low-income students at private, not-for-profit colleges was 66 percent. That's about what it is at Berea in four years.

Neetu Arnold from the conservative National Association of Scholars argued against any increase in Pell grants in an opinion piece in the *Hill* (November 8, 2021) by using Berea data. She wrote, "The main reason Berea students drop out is learning about their academic ability—or lack thereof—during college." Berea staff acknowledge that it is sometimes difficult to differentiate a weak student poorly prepared in a weak high school from a strong student poorly prepared in a weak high school, but Chris Lakes, director of Berea's Office of Student Success and Transition, has a far more nuanced, realistic, and sympathetic perspective about those who leave before graduation.

He and his staff interview every student who leaves, trying to identify academic differences between students who leave and students who graduate. They share their findings with the Admissions Office. Their interviews, plus data collected by the Office of Institutional Research and Assessment, show that the initial SAT or ACT scores of those who finish and those who don't are comparable, and their academic records, for the most part, show success is possible.

President Emeritus Roelofs, a former longtime physics professor at Haverford College and later acting president of Colgate University, said when asked how the Berea students compared to his former students, smiled, and said, "I have had some terrific students at Berea and not so terrific students, just like [at] Haverford."

Lakes explained the reality this way: "Students come in with a can-do attitude and Berea tries hard not to punch them in the face that first year, so our retention rate is strong. But Berea is hard—it's academically difficult, the labor assignments add another challenge, and the expectation of service is always there. We call it 'Berea busy,' and over time acute family issues can grind them down."

Hunger, isolation, illness, housing insecurity, drugs, and domestic abuse linger in impoverished families, haunt those who leave, and often force the students' return home. Poverty is the thread that runs through this reality. Harvard economist Sendhil Mullainathan and Princeton psychologist Eldar Shafir in their book *Scarcity: Why Having Too Little Matters So Much* write that "poverty does not take a vacation. . . . Scarcity directly reduces bandwidth—not a person's inherent capacity, but how much of that capacity is currently available for use."

A powerful example of this came when COVID-19 hit, and Berea gave the students three days to leave.[7] Lakes learned that one of his students would live in a single-wide trailer with twelve other people and was worried that she'd be unable to take Zoom classes. Lakes invited her to join him and his family; she stayed for fourteen months, returned to Berea, and eventually graduated.

"Just last week a student came to see me," Lakes continued. "His grandparents raised him, and his grandmother had just died and there was no one to care for his grandfather. With just six courses to go, he had to drop out and go home. Maybe one day he'll finish at the local community college. I hope so, but his story is all too familiar."

4

LIBERAL ARTS

To offer a high-quality liberal arts education that engages students as they pursue their personal, academic, and professional goals.

In his first year on campus, Chris Thomas Hayes ('06) produced and directed *Hot Chocolate Soul*, a variety show modeled after the famous performances at the Apollo Theater in Harlem. For this one-man show, he wrote and presented hip-hop songs, spoken word poetry, and comedy sketches as well as performed choreographed dances. "We packed the place," he said proudly.

Hayes, the son of a single mother in Hartford, Connecticut, began studying arts administration there at the Hartt School, but, unable to afford to continue, he dropped out. "I doubt if I would have ever returned to college if I had not visited my cousin at Berea," he said. "I knew it was the place for me as soon as I walked on campus."

Berea offers no degree in performing arts administration, but the Second Great Commitment promises to "engage students in their personal, academic, and professional goals." Berea accepted Hayes's credits in music appreciation and management when he transferred from the performing arts conservatory at the start of his sophomore year.

"Berea takes the red tape out of things and lets you, hey, it *wants* you to wander down rabbit holes," Hayes said. That rabbit hole led Chris Hayes eventually to *Sesame Street*.

CONVOCATIONS

Although the most popular majors are career-focused—computer science, biology, business administration, and communication—the Second Great Commitment stresses the importance of a liberal arts education, and has since its earliest days. To that end, Berea has many requirements for all students, including attendance at seven of thirteen convocations offered every semester. Three of those requirements can be at selected theater, music, or dance performances by fellow Bereans each year.

Designed to expand students' intellectual, cultural, and aesthetic experiences, the convocations introduce a wide world to students, few of whom have had such opportunities, and encourage exploration of the new. The students receive information about—and expectations for—proper behavior at the events, attendance is taken, and they are encouraged to ask questions or offer thoughts at the end of each.

Curious about wind instruments? How about the Philadelphia Brass Quintet playing fanfare to jazz? What about reproduction policies in modern China? Ever hear about the Harlan Renaissance?

Gertrude Mbewe ('25), a nursing student from Zambia, arrived at Berea soon after her single mother died unexpectedly and readily admits that she was homesick; however, music has always comforted her, so she makes a point of choosing musical performances. She particularly liked the blind blues singer Jerron Paxton, who sang and played the guitar, a banjo, and a harmonica.

Caedmon Brewer ('24) from Greenup County, Kentucky, majored in political science and remembers well the convocation entitled Conservatives on the Quad.

"I had never thought about a conservative view of college," he said. For his part, Dr. Jonathan Marks, the conservative writer and thinker who gave the lecture, wrote, "I thoroughly enjoyed my visit to Berea. One can feel a rich history . . . and I was really impressed with how they've incorporated convocations into the life of the college."

I attended one convocation with two singers—one white and one Latina. Through expressive dance and bilingual songs, they highlighted the similarities between a Peruvian and an Appalachian grandmother preparing a meal. At the end, a Black student jumped from her seat, enthusiastically waving her hand to be recognized, and said she loved the performance and urged the group to perform it all around Appalachia. "Everyone should see this," she said unequivocally.

TWENTY COURSES OF YOUR CHOICE
OUTSIDE YOUR MAJOR

In addition to seven convocations each semester, every student must take twenty courses outside their major. Tristan Tillery ('24) thought, "Oh, my goodness, that seems like a lot, but now I understand Berea wants us to explore as much as possible, and, in my case, it changed me."

Tillery lived for eight years with his grandparents in northeast Kentucky before they all moved to southern Ohio, where he attended a small private STEM school that gave financial support to low-income students. He entered Berea thinking he'd major in biology and eventually become a psychiatrist.

"But then I took a class on medieval animals. We read fables and studied bestiaries and analyzed how and why the perception of some animals has changed over time. Owls went from being harbingers of death to symbols of wisdom and I began to see myself in history more than in neuroscience." He changed his major to history.

GSTR CLASSES

Within those twenty courses, *every* student must take five general education classes, organized thematically with as many as ten professors from ten different departments teaching in each unit and offering a wide variety of courses, taught through their specific academic lens.

The first two levels both emphasize reasoning, research, and writing college-level essays and papers. The first focuses on critical thinking, and the second focuses on identity and cultural heritage.

In the first one, Chris Hayes, the performing arts major introduced at the start of this chapter, read *Gilgamesh* and *Beowulf* and remembered, "It was a slog. My writing was good, but I couldn't focus on class and the professor knew it."

However, Cansas Dowell ('24), a biology major, named for a television character (pronounced like the state), remembered her first class fondly. She took a class on what constitutes civilization, read novels and ancient texts, and studied archaeological material and art. Professor Rob Foster said the students study "different religious, philosophical, political, and aesthetic systems to . . . understand why humans have upheld the term as an ideal."

"It was cool to learn how similar are some religions," said Dowell, who comes from a devout Christian family in Knoxville, Tennessee. "I liked Buddhism a lot with its focus on love and inner peace, and I was glad to find out that you don't have to be one or another."

Gertrude Mbewe took the course on walking, taught by Professor Jill Bouma from the Sociology Department. They explored all the physical, emotional, political, and spiritual reasons people walk, and for her final paper Mwebe, whose mother had just died, read and analyzed Cheryl Strayed's *Wild: From Lost to Found on the Pacific Crest Trail*.

Suneil Avirneni ('24), a former state high school chess champion and a business major, said, "I thought twenty classes in the liberal arts was incredibly stupid. Now I just think it's excessive." To satisfy his course on identity and heritage, he explored race, gender, class, and education in a history of Berea College.

"I loved reading about John Fee," said this son of a Hindu father who works at a college for women in India and a southern Baptist mother who works in an Oklahoma casino. "A principled radical, Fee sure wasn't like any preacher I have ever met."

In level three, Understanding Christianity, students address Berea's Third Great Commitment and its nonsectarian Christian beliefs that honor its radical legacy. Professor Josh Guthman, a Jewish historian with a scholarly interest in American religious cultures, said, "I want students to see how often unexamined categories of thought and, in this case, religion and Christianity, shape our findings."[1]

"We were all a bit worried that Professor Guthman would tell us what we hear in church about specific beliefs," said Hannah Martin, a sophomore from the town of Berea with long blond hair and cochlear implants. "But on day one, we relaxed."

Martin and fourteen other students were discussing *The Madonna of 115th Street: Faith and Community in Italian Harlem* by Robert Orsi about Italian immigrants to New York City between 1880 and 1950. Guthman pushed the students to react to Orsi's vivid descriptions of the immigrants' practices and how they differed from the formality of traditional churches. He got them to discuss sacred theater from their own experiences and asked why they thought Mary, and not Jesus, figured so prominently in their rituals.

"Maybe mothers have more stature than fathers do in Italian families," Martin suggested.

The students were "doing" cultural anthropology without knowing that's what they were doing, and only at the end of class did Guthman describe Orsi's scholarly methodology. Was he talking about Italian immigrants or Appalachian Baptists or maybe both?

In level four, Scientific Origins, Professor Megan Hoffman explains in one course how the jawbone of a reptile ended up in our ears or why a whale swims the way a dog runs. For his level-four class John Henry Hite III ('19), an agriculture and natural resources major, did independent work on reproduction in rats and nutritional studies of horse feed in Professor Quinn Baptiste's class, and some students in level four take a seminar on contemporary global issues.

LABOR AS AN EXTENSION OF STUDY

Although students do not get academic credit for their labor assignments, those jobs often enrich their majors or, as in the case of Chris Thomas Hayes, the aforementioned performing arts major, lead to a passion and a profession. He worked as an audiovisual editor and media technician in the college's Office of Information Systems and Services; he announced plays and scores at basketball games and "spun records" as a DJ at dances. Then, with a big chunk of his labor earnings, Hayes bought a puppet, Tolly Tucker. Hayes pasted thick black eyebrows on the orange and furry guy, whom Hayes called a "little monster boy." He practiced obsessively, teaching himself to manipulate the "hand and rod" puppet, a style of puppeteering made famous by Jim Henson's Muppets.

"I practiced alone in my dorm room, a bit nervous about being seen as a puppet nerd, although that's what I am," he laughs on the phone from his home in Atlanta. For his senior project in theater, Hayes directed *The Wiz* and stole a little part for Tolly.

"I lay on the floor behind Dorothy's grandparents' couch, moving my hands to control the rods. Tolly popped up and announced all the preperformance details about fire exits and intermission. It was my first-ever public appearance with a puppet."

After graduation, Hayes worked at various theaters and puppet centers. Then the Sesame Workshop, "the Olympics of Puppetry," hired him as an assistant to master puppeteers. That means being a right hand, literally. On his first week at *Sesame Street*, Hayes did the right hand of the frantic electric guitarist, Abby Cadabby. Later, he was the right hand of Elmo, the Count, and Big Bird, and then went from the right hand to the "whole man," doing, among other things, a stint as Hoots the Owl, the legacy puppet famous for his jazzy lecture to Ernie, "Put Down the Duckie."

In 2021, Hayes was cast as Elijah, the wise father to a little boy, Wes, on *Sesame Street*'s new video series for families on racial and cultural distinctiveness. In one episode, a despondent Wes comes home from school with his friend, Abby, and Abby tells Elijah that another kid at school was mean to Wes but that Wes won't talk about it. Elijah puts his left arm around the boy and says that sometimes when we have "big feelings" it helps to breathe, let your emotions go, and then share. All three Muppets then do some deep belly breaths with their chests going up and down and their mouths opening, in sync, to exhale.

"Sometimes we feel hurt in our bodies," Elijah says.

"I feel it in my stomach, Dad," admits Wes.

"What would you say to the person who hurt your feelings?" Elijah asks.

"I'd say I feel sad because curry chicken is my favorite food, and he shouldn't laugh at it," says Wes. Now that Wes has told Elijah what troubles him—and with Abby's support—Wes feels "strong."

To perform this skit, all three puppeteers lie on specially made, whisper-quiet, short rolling platforms—called "butt carts." With one hand, they manipulate the rod that controls their respective character's arms. With the other hand, they each manipulate their puppet's chest and mouth as they recite their lines and ad-lib occasionally. As they each attentively watch a small monitor in front of them to help synchronize their movements, they bring their characters to life.

"Puppetry on TV is the biggest 'pat your head and rub your stomach' test of all and can drive you crazy sometimes," Hayes says.

Hayes said that Tolly, his labor purchase, his African American history classes, and his student trip to Ghana all make it now possible for him, one of the few Black members of the show, "to pump a ton of my own personality and experiences into Elijah." Thousands of kids have watched Elijah and his son, Wes.

THE INTENSITY OF A SOCIAL JUSTICE WARRIOR

Alice Driver's ('03) trajectory differs dramatically from Chris Hayes's, but, as with Hayes, Driver identified her passions at Berea. Born in 1983, Alice was raised in Oark, a tiny town in Northwest Arkansas where her parents, a potter and a weaver, were part of the back-to-the-land movement in the 1970s when some two thousand to six thousand urban idealists flocked to the Ozark Mountains. Land was inexpensive, nature expansive, and urban degradation distant.

"If you own your own land, you control your own destiny," her father often said.

Committed to a simple and sustainable existence, the family lived in a hand-built house with a two-seat outhouse thirty miles from the nearest town. Alice grew up running in the dense woods, spotting snakes, and swimming in the white water of the rocky Mulberry River. Her family was neither conservative nor religious—unlike her Pentecostal high school friends—but they were socially conscious and, like their rural neighbors, believed that love, forgiveness, and the Golden Rule are the three important things in the Bible.

"When I got to Berea, it felt like home . . . it was my parents' ideal in an educational setting."

She signed up for Spanish and, by her own admission, was terrible at it until Berea made it possible for her to spend a summer with a Mexican family in Morelia in the central state of Michoacán. Back at Berea, her Spanish professor then urged her to use her "still-stunted language skills" to help struggling Mexican immigrants locally, and Alice was hooked.

"My commitment to social justice started with my nontraditional upbringing and was reinforced at Berea with its commitment to service and its encouragement for me to write." Some of that encouragement came from Nikki Finney, the poet, who was once a visiting professor at Berea.

"I kept in touch with her over the years," Alice said, "and she wrote me something I've never forgotten: 'So much of the world needs the muscle found in true words. Please keep sending what your head and belly make as one loaf.'"

Upon graduation, Driver earned a master's and then a PhD in Hispanic studies at the University of Kentucky, primarily, she explained, as a gateway into journalism. In 2017, the University of Arizona Press published *More or Less Dead: Feminicide, Haunting, and the Ethics of Representation in Mexico*, her dissertation on violence against women in Mexico and how those deaths are discounted or ignored. Like Hayes, Driver is disciplined and persistent.

While doing research for her dissertation, Driver met a trans woman in El Salvador who, like others, had been beaten by gang members and was planning on seeking asylum at the US-Mexican border. Driver joined her on her trek north. After riding rickety public buses through El Salvador and crossing the Suchiate River to Mexico on a raft, they arrived at the US border. The trans woman was held for seven months in a male detention camp as Driver found advocates back in the States to take her asylum case. Successful, the El Salvadoran woman now lives in San Diego with a new name, a new job, and new English skills—and Driver jump-started her career as a journalist, focusing on human rights and labor.

Driver is now back in Arkansas, writing about the migrants who work in a massive Tyson chicken processing plant in Northwest Arkansas. The company's public relations machines are forceful, and their influence is deep with politicians and media, even as serious allegations of exploitation of workers swirl. Traditional journalists— and, most recently, the Union of Concerned Scientists—report the data; Driver will tell their stories in a book that Astra House will publish in 2024.

LIBERAL ARTS ENRICH

The headline of the Berea story might be no tuition, but the promise of Berea goes far deeper than that. As the Second Great Commitment states, Berea helps low-income students identify their passions and their talents—whether it be a hand-and-rod puppet or a laptop and a chord—and it does so with a grounding in the liberal arts. In 2022, the *Washington Monthly* released its annual ratings of private four-year liberal arts colleges, using its three equally weighted criteria—social mobility, the research accomplishments of students, and a commitment to community and national service. The magazine rated Berea the fifth-best four-year liberal arts college in the entire United States.[2]

Students in a math class. Courtesy of student photographer Arnold O'Neil/ Berea College.

5

INCLUSIVE CHRISTIAN VALUES

To stimulate understanding of the Christian faith and its many expressions and to emphasize the Christian ethic and the motive of service to others.

Berea is not a Bible college; it is not affiliated with any Christian denomination, it follows none of the rules or precepts of Protestant or Catholic faiths, and it seeks to convert no one. Nonetheless, I approached the Third Great Commitment like a stranger in a foreign land with doubts about its beauty.

I arrived on campus one Sunday afternoon to spend a week exploring Berea's nonsectarian Christian commitment. That afternoon two young men, Ben Leis and Tongtu Zechar, were sitting in the sun on the steps of the Hutchins Library. I introduced myself, saying I had been to campus many times, interviewing students, faculty, and staff, attending classes, reading in the archives, and now was back to explore Berea's commitment to nonsectarian Christianity.

"Berea leans too far from its Christian heritage and should just drop it," Ben Leis ('21) said definitively. The son of Protestant missionaries in Japan, Leis was currently exploring Catholicism and said he was bothered by the lack of Christian symbols on campus.

"They even took the cross out of the logo," he said.

Tongtu Zechar ('22) disagreed, quietly but forthrightly saying that his faith in God saved him at the lowest point in his life. "I believe," he said, "that Berea's Christian identity is why it's such an accepting place."

Zechar said he was adopted by a couple in Louisville eight years before, when he was twelve. With a speech impediment and apparent cleft lip, he must have had a rough time in his younger years. But there we were openly discussing personal faith on a college campus, something that certainly did not happen in my college days.

What I came to realize is that today's Berea College embraces the aspirations of the fundamental teachings of Jesus and honors its founder's deep faith in what he called "impartial love." The college seeks to help students understand the ethics of its founder's determination and Christianity as a historical, global movement. The college also encourages the development of the students' spiritual lives by helping them in class and out of class connect those values to relationships, both personal and cultural, and to start to identify one's purpose in life.

FEE'S LEGACY

John Fee rejected the idea that the rules and structures of a church—any church—define faith or spiritualty. He believed *the* essential Christian value is love thy neighbor as thyself, which informed his abolitionist commitment and his devotion to equality between Blacks and white people. His fellow Presbyterian ministers—until he left their fellowship—railed against adultery, lying, and stealing but never condemned owning, leasing, or trading Black people. Fee found that duplicity despicable, and his radical faith during the deadliest time in our history fueled his courage.

Fee had made little progress convincing people of the evils of slavery when his tiny church in Lewis County, Kentucky, voted unanimously to declare slaveholding a sin and to refuse membership to any slaveholder. The regional governing body of the Presbyterian Church, the synod, heard about Fee's church's action and was appalled. When the synod met in Paris, Kentucky, in October 1845,

John Fee attended the meeting for the first time and was roundly criticized.[1]

The synod members demanded that Fee follow the rules of the church and allow slaveholders to worship in his church, but Fee pushed back, saying, "Anything in the principle or practice of a church member, which is contrary to the Word of God, violates the law of love."

"If the young man shall find himself one day taken out, ridden on a rail and dunked in a pond, he need not be surprised," another minister responded before his colleagues voted to censure Fee's actions.

Fee defiantly ignored the synod's edict and, with his parishioners, continued the practice. When the synod next met, the members returned to Fee's insubordination.

"It is your *duty* to construe the constitution of the church as the body you belong to construes it!" one angry minister bellowed.

"It is manifest that my work with you is done," Fee countered forcefully. Refusing to give the church hierarchy more respect than the word of Christ, he left the Presbyterian Church, never to return. He and his family paid a high price for his fierce advocacy, but John and Matilda Fee never wavered in the gospel of impartial love and inclusion, never bending to power, profit, or conformity.

BEREA'S MOTTO

Later, when Fee and his colleagues signed the first formal charter for Berea College, it read in part, "This college shall be under an influence strictly Christian and, as such, be opposed to sectarianism, slaveholding, caste and every other wrong institution or practice."

To this day, Berea College remains a nonsectarian Christian college, unaffiliated with any denomination and defining its philosophy with the motto it adopted in 1866: "God has made of one blood all peoples of the earth."[2]

That motto still resonates with LaQuita Middletown ('04). As a child, Middletown was in and out of foster care in Birmingham, Alabama, and now, a published poet and spoken word performer, she also teaches anger management to traumatized teenagers at a Christian social service agency in Houston. She noted, "People are surprised that as an outspoken, politically active Black woman, I would be guided by that motto, but that is the only way we'll make the world better. I always keep it in my head."

PERIODIC REVIEW

Berea has grappled with this commitment and has made changes to it periodically. Mandatory chapel, for instance, stopped in 1973. Ben Leis is correct; the official college logo no longer contains a cross, and as Appalachia diversified demographically and the college's commitment to international students grew, Berea strengthened its interfaith programming. A few students, particularly Catholics, believe that some on campus feel alienated, and one student cited the issue of abortion. He alleged that one year prolife students displayed vivid photographs of aborted fetuses at a college fair, and when others complained the college, purportedly, made the students cover the photographs.

Under President Larry Shinn (1994–2012), a broadly representative college committee undertook a comprehensive review to reassess the validity and usefulness of all the commitments, including the third. Its report, *Being and Becoming*, reaffirmed the college's historic Christian identity and its goal "to foster a fellowship of inclusive, faithful, and life-altering values," or, as Fee declared, "impartial love." In 2013, in another review, some language was tweaked, and the commitments reaffirmed. The commitments are posted around campus and referred to regularly, and when potential administrative and faculty staff are interviewed for jobs, they are often asked which commitment is their favorite. I began to ask, too. Reverend LeSette Wright, dean of the chapel and the Willis D. Weatherford, Jr. Campus Christian Center, puts the commitment in historical terms. "We should always acknowledge our elders as we are, after all, standing on their shoulders." Luke Hodson ('02), Associate Vice President of Admissions, leans toward the first and its commitment to Appalachia. Ashley Cochrane from the Center for Excellence in Learning Through Service likes them best when seen as one. Samson Kitenda ('23), a political science major from Cincinnati, likes them all and says unequivocally, "I have never been anywhere where everyone feels comfortable and coexists so well with both politics and religion."

GEOGRAPHY IS DESTINY, TOO

Berea's adherence to nonsectarian Christianity springs, in part, from Fee's dedication and, in part, from Berea's location, its regional focus, and, hence, its students' backgrounds. Although in 2020 almost 78 percent of the students identified as mainstream Protestant, a few identified as Catholic, Hindu, Muslim, or Buddhist, and a growing number considered themselves atheist, agnostic, or "None" (people who have no religious affiliation). Another 21 percent identified as "Other Christian." Judith Weckman, former director of the Office of Institutional Research and Assessment, defines "Other Christian" as members of the many tiny, independent churches that dot Appalachia as well as the evangelical megachurches.[3]

Wide gulfs often exist between these denominations— Missionary Baptists differ from Free Will Baptists, Union Baptists differ from Primitive Baptists, followers of the African Methodist Episcopal Church differ from members of the Christian Methodist

Episcopal Church, who differ from the National Baptist Convention. They all believe in God and the importance of family, but the underlying principles can differ profoundly and engender debate and, sometimes, strife.

Is life predestined or does free will matter? Does God choose his people and, thus, missionary work is wrongheaded? Does prayer bring prosperity? Practices differ dramatically, too. Does snake handling prove that God will protect you no matter what? Does the degree of the preachers' passion matter? What about talking in tongues or the laying of hands? What about the role of women in the church? What about homosexuality? These are knotty questions, exacerbated today by hyper partisan politics.

"I am not religious, but I came here, in part, to honor a saintly man who was a Berea graduate and lived in my North Carolina mountain town," said Matthew Woodward ('21), a young man with green hair and pink nail polish. "When I first came, I lied and did not tell the college that I was a drug addict. By the end of my first year, I had flunked out, went home, got clean, and reapplied. This time I told the truth, and Berea let me back in. I think Christianity is kinda unspoken on campus, but the college is kind to us and shows us how to live—and isn't that Christianity?"

DANFORTH CHAPEL

The most visible illustration of Berea's Christian commitment is Danforth Chapel. Built with Indiana limestone and walnut-stained oak, the simple, small chapel, bare of any iconography save for one wooden cross, was deliberately attached to Draper Building, the main classroom building. Together they underscore Berea's dual commitment to educational and spiritual growth.

"How is this different from a church or a synagogue, a mosque or a temple, or a Wiccan on a midnight hilltop," President Lyle Roelofs

Draper Hall and Danforth Chapel. Courtesy of student photographer Jay Buckner/Berea College.

(2012–2023) asked from the platform in the Danforth Chapel on the fiftieth anniversary of Berea's Campus Christian Center. "Religious observances do happen here, and the spiritual quest we are all on is furthered, but here also happens deep integration of faith and other forms of learning and knowledge . . . and that is the real point of our Third Great Commitment."

William Danforth, a wealthy businessman from St. Louis, joined Berea's board of trustees in 1922, finding its educational mission, its Labor Program, and its commitment to Christian values compelling. He proceeded to donate stock; pay for specific needs, such as the funeral of a tragically killed student; and even offered to send President Francis Hutchins (1939–1967) on a cruise. (Hutchins refused, unwilling to leave campus for two months.)

Danforth, founder of Ralston Purina, was what today we'd call a straight arrow. Born in 1870 in a small town in rural Missouri, he was a sickly child who grew up to be a shrewd entrepreneur and a health aficionado who sought balance between his physical, mental, social, and religious lives. "Think tall, smile tall, live tall, and stand tall" was his personal motto.

In 1938, he donated all the money needed to build Danforth Chapel at Berea. It was the first of twenty-four nondenominational chapels he built on college campuses, from Morehouse College to the University of Iowa.

"The Danforth Chapel program," writes Margaret Grubiak, an architectural historian, "offered an early model of how to make religion available within communities that needed to respect religious differences."

CAMPUS CHRISTIAN CENTER

Established in 1971 when Willis Weatherford Jr. (1967–1984) was president and endowed by Eli Lilly, the pharmaceutical magnate, the Campus Christian Center extends Berea's understanding of Christianity and nurtures interfaith dialogue. Every Tuesday, for instance, one of the college chaplains assumes responsibility for a thirty-minute service in the chapel for anyone who would like to attend and then eat lunch together. At one such service in February 2022, a student chaplain read a passage from the Bible, the Berea College Bluegrass Ensemble sang "Keep Your Eyes on the Prize," and Silas House, Berea associate professor of Appalachian studies, novelist, and a gay man, gave a brief sermon. It went, in part:

> That song was first sung . . . in the 1950s, yet here we are still, aiming for that prize . . . still holding on to the plow. Our eyes fixed on the prize . . . many of us still do not have equity. . . .

Yes, there is plenty to make us angry and frustrated and even scared. . . . I struggle with anger, frustration, and fear all the time. But what helps me more than anything is latching on to the joy and the wonder . . . to be a person who is protecting myself while also giving grace to others, always looking for the holiness in myself, and in everyone around me. Keep your eyes on the prize.

Two days later, and every Thursday, the Campus Christian Center invites a leader from another church or a different faith to talk over lunch with anyone curious. Recently a second-generation Bahá'í, who graduated from Berea many years before, spoke about the joy he experienced getting to know the first Tibetan Buddhist students at the college.

STUDENT CHAPLAINS

Each year, the Campus Christian Center accepts up to seventeen students as student chaplains for their labor assignments. Among their many assignments, these student chaplains help organize the weekly events. In 2022, the student chaplains included several practicing Christians, one Hindu, and one Wiccan.

Once accepted, the student chaplains attend a ten-day workshop on campus in August. They hear from the directors of all the college's student services, and most importantly, they are taught to listen and ask open-ended questions as they get to know other students. The student chaplains are not missionaries but emotional supports to their peers. They are not psychologists but learn how to ask for help from others and how to make a referral for a student sensitively; they learn the difference between privacy and confidentiality. They work fifteen hours a week, not the standard ten, and must organize two special events a year.

Half of the student chaplains will be assigned to first-year dormitories, where, along with student resident advisers, they will get to know each new student and build a sense of community. Cansas Dowell ('24), the girl who loved her general studies class on civilization, was a student chaplain majoring in biology with an interest in marine science. One of the two events she hosted was a showing of the movie *Jaws* followed by a discussion she led.

"It was a full house. Afterwards we talked about our collective and somewhat irrational fear of sharks, and I told them about how important sharks are to the ecology of the sea."

Other student chaplains focus on what for many students is a difficult transition. Matthew Graham ('19) sat in a classroom every evening for two hours, Monday through Friday, where students could drop by for snacks and a chat. He detailed his reasoning: "I tried my best to get them to let out what they were holding in. Between classes, homework, and work, time management is always a big issue at Berea. We also worry about our sisters and brothers, dads, and mothers. We're eating at college, but maybe no one is back home."

The following years, Matthew Graham fulfilled his labor requirements in the Athletic Department. "As a high school basketball player, I wanted to experience that side of Berea, too, so I applied to be the college reporter for the women's volleyball and softball teams. I wrote articles on the bus coming home from games, and I loved it," he said enthusiastically. "Now my ambition is to put it all together—service and athletics—and eventually work with Missionary Athletics International."

A-Nya Badger ('23), a psychology major from Dunbar, West Virginia, who calls herself Thena, concocted from Aphrodite and Athena, does not come from a particularly religious family, although her mother occasionally attends a Holiness Church and her grandmother was a Southern Baptist. She became a student chaplain, but faith had little to do with it. Rather, she said, "I recognized that the job gave me the freedom and creativity to help students, particularly queer ones, who probably have been emotionally and spiritually derided all their lives." In 2022, she was one of four gay student chaplains. "I help people process hurt. I cannot prepare people not to be hurt, but I can help them toughen their skin and set boundaries. To walk away, if necessary," she explained.

Ben Leis, the son of Protestant missionaries in Japan whom I met on the library steps, was not an active participant in the Campus Christian Center, but he respected most of the student chaplains he knew. "They often provide a safe space for others, but it's tough to be present and not crushed by the burden of hardship that is sometimes shared with them."

UNDERSTANDING CHRISTIANITY IN GSTR 310

The integration of faith and learning happens in many ways at Berea, from star mapping in the forest to encouraging individual stewardship of the earth, and it happens in the classrooms. With another nod to its radical Christian roots, Berea requires *all* students, from biology to business majors and from English to engineering majors, to take General Studies 310, Understanding Christianity.

Taught by ten different professors from the History, Philosophy, Religious Studies, and Sociology Departments, the course description states that "the students will imagine and consider Christianity from both inside and outside the faith, from vantages of various disciplines, as an instance of the great phenomenon of religion, and as a way of understanding life's purpose and meaning that remains important to two billion people around the world."

Professor Steve Gowler, a practicing Christian, begins his 310 class with Tolstoy's autobiographical essay, "A Confession." Born into the Russian Orthodox Church, Tolstoy left the church and then in middle age, having gained fame, fortune, and a family, pondered the meaning of life.

"Tolstoy gives the students permission to ask their own questions about life," Professor Gowler explained. "They read about and discuss the ways Christianity has been expressed in belief and practice, moral values and actions, and in different communities," he told me as we sat at a small table in front of the Boone Tavern Hotel on a warm spring day.

Kayla Boyd ('24), the only child of a single mother who works as a janitor in Southwest Virginia, is not religious but does say she tries to be spiritual. She took Professor Gowler's class, and when I asked her why she thought the college did not require a class on Understanding Judaism or Understanding Islam, she replied, "If Fee had been Jewish, we'd be studying its basic values and its variations, too. Same if he had been a Muslim."

To encourage close reading of texts, Gowler's students write eight short papers and one long research paper on a significant topic in Christian history, theology, or practice, approved by Gowler. In the spring of 2022, those topics included "Christian Anarchism and Violence," "Christianity and White Supremacy," "Jesus on Stage: *Jesus Christ Superstar* and *Godspell*," and "Solitude and Spirituality in Christianity and Hinduism."

Caedmon Brewer ('24), a political science major, who never went to Danforth Chapel or participated in Campus Christian Center activities, really enjoyed 310, thinking it made him more self-reflective. His final paper was titled "The Merciless Battle between the Spiritual and the Flesh: Understanding Scorsese and Kazantzakis's Portrayals of Jesus."

SPIRITUAL MUSIC AND SPIRITUAL TALK EVERYWHERE

Some 67 percent of Berea students participate in some music program, ranging from bel canto singers to a mariachi band. The long-standing Berea Concert Choir has sixty singers, chosen annually through auditions, who perform both sacred and secular music on campus and as far away as Barcelona and Beijing. The Bluegrass Ensemble, usually five or six instrumentalists and often a singer or two, also performs on campus and has toured internationally. In 2016, CBS highlighted both groups when it chose Berea for its traditional Christmas Eve special. Students sang and played instruments, and behind the scenes, other students handled all the technical aspects of the hour-long broadcast.

But nothing is more "uniquely Berean," said President Roelofs, than the piece called "River Medley." Shot at the college's large auditorium and outdoors on the campus, and now available on YouTube, the Concert Choir and the Blue Grass Ensemble blend classical choral music with bluegrass and Negro spirituals, using three traditional hymns: "On Jordan's Stormy Bank," "As I Went Down to the River to Pray," and "Shall We Gather at the River." It is a disciplined, diverse group of singers and instrumentalists with different skills and different perspectives, amplifying each other and yet operating as a single unit to move people.

But one does not need to take a class or attend a performance to fall into full discussions of spirituality and religion on campus as I did that Sunday afternoon with Leis and Zechar or another day when I met Josh Boone ('21) in the library.

He was working on his capstone project in American history about the economic drivers behind the pirates who terrorized sailors off North and South Carolina in the eighteenth century. Boone grew up in Jackson, Mississippi, where his father homeschooled him for eight years. Once a week, he and two friends, all Pentecostals, meet to discuss the Bible. He invited me to join them.

We met in the lobby of the Boone Tavern, named for Daniel Boone, but no relation to Josh. I listened, unable to follow their lively debate over which Bible verses predict the Rapture, and they patiently answered my questions about the significance of talking in tongues; there, too, they disagreed on its meaning. But there was agreement when I asked what they thought about Berea.

"When I was accepted, I spent three weeks praying as I was not sure I should leave my sick father, and then I decided to come," Josh said. "I love Berea because Berea loves its students, all its students."

His friend, Aaron Stover ('21), grew up in Martinsburg, West Virginia. Married to another student, the daughter of missionaries in Africa, and studying child and family services, Aaron said, "I like Berea's religious diversity. Before I came, I had never been challenged in my faith, and now I have agency to choose."

LOSING FAITH AT BEREA

I wondered if some students who come with faith lose it at Berea. After all, it is one of the concerns potential parents express. Not surprisingly, the opinions vary. Ethan Hamblin ('14), a gay activist from eastern Kentucky, said, "Oh, no, honey. Many stay with it, including me." Alex Gibson ('08), the biracial former president of the Student Government Association, replied point blank, "I never met a Pentecostal at Berea who stayed a Pentecostal." Chapman Evans ('22), who was not active in the Campus Christian Center but also found Berea too secular at times, now explores Orthodox Christianity. But my favorite story rests with Ashley Long Seals ('08) and her close friend, Josh Noah ('08), neither of whom have lost their faith.

Ashley Long Seals majored in Appalachian studies and was the lead singer in the Berea Bluegrass Ensemble. Brought up in a deeply Christian family in Lee County, Virginia, Long Seals went home after her graduation to establish an anti-littering program at the county's Department of Public Works and then ran its tourism office. She also returned to her family's Holiness Church, where the women and men sit separately, snakes in wooden boxes are always present, and the singing is joyous. She married a young widower with three boys under the age of five, and together they had two more little boys. They now live in a small town about thirty miles from Birmingham, where her husband supervises mining inspectors for the federal government and she teaches three-year-old children with autism.

"Luckily, I found a Holiness Church near us where I feel at home," she said on the phone during a break in her workday.

Pentecostal Holiness churches condemn homosexuality, writing, "We have maintained a strong position against premarital, extramarital, and deviant sex, including homosexual and lesbian relationships, refusing to accept the loose moral standards of our society."

But that did not—and has not—disrupted the friendship between Ashley Long Seals and Josh Noah. Noah grew up in Mount Airy, North Carolina, where his father, now retired, worked in a factory making airplane seats and his mother, a charismatic Pentecostal, homeschooled him and several siblings. When he turned seventeen, never having thought about college, Noah joined the Melody Boys from Arkansas, an old-time gospel quartet, as the group's baritone. They traveled the country to conventions and festivals, including the Grand Ole Gospel Reunion and his favorite, the National Quartet Convention. "People in more conservative church groups follow these singing groups, kind of like the rest of the world follows pop singers . . . I grew up following it, too, so it was a highlight to sing there," he wrote.

But Noah knew he was gay and did not know how he would fare in that world, and not wanting to find out, he quit and returned home, still in the closet. He attended two different community colleges and then enrolled at Berea. He immediately joined the Black Music Ensemble, the Concert Choir, and the Bluegrass Ensemble, where Ashley Long sang soprano. They became fast friends and, like Ashley, Noah majored in Appalachian studies, saying, "I wanted to understand the region, my religious background, myself, and my parents rather than just belittling it all and walking away."

Noah also fell hard for a fellow student and came out of the closet. "Berea made that easy for me," he said.

At their graduation in 2008, Dr. Ben Carson, at that time a professor of pediatric neurosurgery at Johns Hopkins University, gave the commencement speech and then Josh Noah, playing the piano with sparse grace, and Ashley Long, standing straight with her long brown hair, sang together the soulful song "The Prayer," made famous by Andrea Bocelli and Celine Dion, to the large, rapt audience.

While Ashley moved back home, Josh went on for a PhD in cultural anthropology and then moved to Beijing for five years as a teacher in a bilingual international school. When COVID-19 hit, he went traveling, earning his living with online tutoring for Chinese students. When we spoke, he was in Macedonia before exploring the rest of the Balkans. His parents know he's gay, and although they have never accepted his sexuality, he's okay with that. "I don't seek to change them, and they won't change me," he explained.

As for Ashley, she tells me, "We had a wonderful friendship. We laughed. We cried. We traveled. We sang. We had a blast. All the while we had two completely different beliefs. Two separate lifestyles, and we loved each other."

There's that impartial love again. It worked for bell hooks, too. The daughter of an impoverished Black family in Kentucky, a graduate of Stanford University and the University of Wisconsin, a former teacher at several elite institutions, and the widely published feminist writer, hooks chose to spend the last decade of her life at Berea. When she died in 2021, she left behind the bell hooks center, many students and staff she had inspired, and all her papers.

As she said in an interview with Helen Tworkov, "if I were really asked to define myself, I wouldn't start with race; I wouldn't start with blackness; I wouldn't start with gender; I wouldn't start with feminism. I would start with stripping down to what fundamentally informs my life, which is that I'm a seeker on the path. . . . But where I stand spiritually is, steadfastly, on a path about love."[4]

6

LEARNING THROUGH LABOR
AND SERVICE

To promote learning and serving in the community through the student Labor Program, honoring the dignity and utility of all work, mental and manual, and taking pride in work well done.

Taylor Miles ('20) grew up in the Bible Belt of North Carolina "in a town with no streetlights, but hundreds of waterfalls." A tall, open, and friendly young woman, she did well in high school, but life at home was tough. Her father was an alcoholic and her stepmother often forced her to skip school to care for her grandchildren. Miles ran away, and the police eventually listed her as homeless. She ended up living with a kind teacher, who told her about Berea. Taylor applied as an emancipated youth and was accepted. She said, "I loved the idea of working for my college degree and I wanted to be far away from home." Assigned her first year to work on the college farm, she returned there every year and ended up majoring in agriculture and natural resources.

THE BEREA COLLEGE FARM

In 1871, Berea had a few dairy cows that grazed on two acres of land at the bottom of the ridge. Now the Berea farm, still at the bottom of the ridge, covers over 512 acres of highly diversified land. With the growing interest in locally grown food, overall wellness, and environmental concerns, about eighty colleges now offer students small vegetable plots and courses in relevant disciplines, but Berea, with the oldest continually worked college farm in America, is one of the few that offers an undergraduate degree in agriculture.[1]

With pastureland for cattle, goats, and pigs; row crops of corn, wheat, and alfalfa; and eighty-five acres of US Department of Agriculture–certified organic produce, the Berea College Farm continually evolves. The poultry operation closed for financial reasons, but the farm won certification for its animal welfare protocols; tobacco is no longer grown, but the Berea College Farm Store is opened every day and students from various departments bake, make, market, and sell organic fruit and vegetables, meats and sausages, pastries, cookies, and even kombucha.

The Berea farm and farm store serve as a labor assignment for some, an educational laboratory for others, and a demonstration farm for many. The Clark Chair in Mountain Agriculture and former director of the farm Sean Clark (no relation) says, "Our goal is to

Students working on the Berea farm. Courtesy of Justin Skeens.

help students go from seed to market with an environmental ethic at all times."

HOW THE LABOR PROGRAM BEGAN

As industrialization in America accelerated, people worried about the growing schism between workers and intellectuals. In 1833, the Society for Promoting Manual Labor in Literary Institutions published a detailed argument for combining work with study. Theodore Weld, hired by the society, wrote the treatise and then, with its support, traveled beyond the Alleghany Mountains to lecture about the idea and search for a divinity school to adopt its principles. He found it at Lane Theological Seminary, where Reverend Lyman Beecher had incorporated the approach into the divinity school he led. Weld enrolled at Lane.[2]

When John Fee entered Lane in 1842, he worked three hours a day at its printing press, and other students (all men) built roads and delivered mud to the brick shop. In his autobiography, Fee never mentions the labor aspects of his study, but when he and his colleague John Rogers envisioned a school, they saw manual labor as a way for students unable to afford an education to get one.

The original charter read in part, "The purpose of the college shall be to furnish the facilities for a thorough education to all persons of good moral character, at least possible expense, and all the inducements and facilities for manual labor which can be reasonably supplied by the Board of Trustees shall be offered." The founders did not see labor as an integral part of a well-rounded education as Berea does today.

Berea's first president, E. Henry Fairchild (1869–1889), enjoyed supervising student workers, but he worried that without dedicated supervisors and educational relevance such labor made little sense.[3] William B. Stewart succeeded Fairchild, but soon left, and was followed by William Frost (1892–1920).

In 1892 when Frost accepted the position, he not only convinced the board to eliminate tuition for all students but also strongly defended "productive industry" for them. He proceeded to build on the industries Berea already had and introduce new opportunities. In 1910, the school mandated work for every student.

Work assignments have evolved, multiplied, and imprinted themselves on the college, in the community of Berea, and, in some cases, across wider Appalachia. There are more than 125 different job categories, from designing and running a STEM camp for local middle school students to managing all the solid waste and recycling sites or serving as a teaching assistant in the Chemistry Department. Work is considered a crucial part of the Berea experience, and with free tuition plus labor salaries, many students graduate with little or no debt.[4]

HOW LABOR WORKS?

Berea outlines the goals for its Labor Program as democratizing and honoring *all* work well done. There is no stigma attached to manual work, no class distinctions exist between white- and blue-collar jobs; it does not matter if you are washing floors or doing research in the archives. What matters is how well you assume responsibility for doing a good job. The labor positions build professionalism and confidence in students, who gain the soft skills—and sometimes the exact skills—that many companies and organizations need.

Upon enrollment, all Berea students sign an agreement promising to work—some operational and some academic, some manual, some cerebral. The contract lays out what is expected and the consequences of not fulfilling those expectations.

Legally, work colleges—and there are nine members of the consortium—must require *every* student to work and get paid for a minimum of ten hours a week. All jobs pay $6.09 an hour to start and increase to as much as $9.50 an hour as students assume more responsibility, master more skills, or work holidays. The labor supervisor, who might be a faculty or administrative staff member, guides and evaluates the students, and when the students graduate, they take with them both academic and labor transcripts.

During students' first year, the college assigns the labor positions, based on a form that the students submit outlining their work and volunteer history. Those jobs are in the dining hall, on the farm, in Student Craft, or in facilities. In the following year, the students apply for their labor positions, listed and described on the college website.

"I have never had a better prepared and responsible employee right out of college," said the chief development officer at the University of Iowa, referring to a recent Berea graduate whose final labor assignment had been in the fundraising office at Berea.

FINANCES OF THE LABOR PROGRAM

The student Labor Program decreases the operating costs for the college, as students provide more than 16,500 hours per week on campus at wages lower than the minimum wage. (Thirty-six percent of the students work more than ten hours a week.) These savings, of course, are offset somewhat by the cost of running the Labor Program.

Overall management of the Labor Program is like running a human resource office for part-time staff with ever-changing schedules for a host of different businesses. The labor supervisors are some of the busiest people on campus. Students must be taught and supervised, their work schedules determined, hours confirmed, pay authorized, and grades given.

Individual class schedules dictate when a student can work, and that changes day by day. Efficiency is challenging, particularly if a site, for instance, offers products for sale, like the farm store or the Student Craft program, and steady production can be problematic. In the 1930s, Berea's nationally known Candy Kitchen sold peanut brittle, fruitcakes, and decorated tea sugars, but it closed for good in 1970 when handmade candy could not compete with mass-produced candy. Today, it might be hard to get pastries baked in time for breakfast at the farm store if the student responsible on Mondays and Wednesdays has an 8:00 a.m. class or no students are available for the lunch rush. Likewise, first-year students in Student Craft must first be taught how to weave blankets or knot broomcorn before orders can be filled. The finance people would love to see profits increase with lowered expenses, but the labor supervisors are at the mercy of academic demands. The Student Craft program, for instance, costs approximately $650,000 a year to operate and realizes about $475,000 in sales.

Derrick Singleton, Vice President of Operations and Sustainability, remains hopeful that all Berea enterprises succeed, but admits that "it is very difficult to run a production company with stop, start, stop, start workers' hours, and I understand that crafts are key to 'teaching the hands.' They are great public relations and make terrific donor gifts." If there is tension between profit and learning, it appears friendly and mutually respectful.

THE ROOTS OF STUDENT CRAFT AT BEREA

First-year students do not get a choice—that will come later. Thirty will go to the Student Craft program to learn about Appalachian cultural traditions, master a skill, and gain the satisfaction of possibly selling their products.

"I never knew slaves couldn't marry until I came to Berea," said a first-year Black student twirling a long-handled broom in a Rube Goldberg contraption in the bay window of the college bookstore. "Now I am making the kind of broom they would have jumped over to signify their love," and then, unprompted, she added, "I love Berea."

She continued to bind tightly the naturally dyed broomcorn bristles to the twisted wood handle. Once approved, her broom will be for sale at the college bookstore, online, or at the Log House Craft Gallery, all delivered with her name on a tag.

The Student Craft program started at Berea when President Frost bought coverlets made by women in the mountains as gifts for donors up north. They were popular, and he ordered many from the women.

One woman told him, "President Frost, . . . to make so many kivers (covers) we will have to raise more sheep, shear them, pick and wash the wool, card it and spin it, then collect the bark . . . to color it. Then we will have to have the loom all set up, fix the warp, and beam it, then get a draft, and thread the warp for the pattern we want, and then we will be ready for weaving. . . . It's no child's play to weave a kiver, president."

The famous Fireside Industries at Berea were born. The artisans soon won attention, respect, and awards at the Paris and Buffalo expositions, and exhibits in New York, all of which helped attract donors. Then somewhere, presumably in New York on a fundraising trip, President Frost met Candace Wheeler, the social wife of a wealthy businessman.

Wheeler loved the Arts and Crafts movement, which prized the beauty and value of handmade household items, simple in form, affordable in price, and related to nature, either through material or design.[5] Aligned with the tony New York Society of Decorative Arts (NYSDA), Wheeler also had a democratic streak and social consciousness. In 1878, she had begun the first Women's Exchange in New York. Unlike the peer-reviewed exhibits at the NYSDA, the Women's Exchange was open to any female artisan—no matter how humble the product or unschooled the artist.[6] In 1901, Wheeler visited Berea and urged President Frost to embed a crafts program into the school to keep the traditions alive. It took a decade, but then President Frost hired Anna Ernberg, who did just that.

"We do not wish to introduce new forms of weaving . . . but to encourage and develop the forms handed down by tradition," President Frost wrote to her.

A talented Swedish-born weaver, Ernberg had immigrated to the United States and taught in New York before moving to Berea in 1911. Soon she was traveling into the mountains by mule and horseback, meeting the women and appreciating the richness of the mountains' natural resources. Over time she used the wood, willows, corn husks, and flax to build a vibrant crafts program for students, adding ceramics, broom craft, and woodworking. By the mid-1920s, Ernberg was working with more than 400 students and more than 150 family weavers. In 1930, Ida Tarbell, a journalist, published a widely circulated list of the fifty most influential women in America; Anna Ernberg was on the list.

STUDENT CRAFT TODAY

Aaron Beale, a thin, bald, and bearded man, a furniture maker by training with a degree in labor history, directs the Student Craft program, leading it into the future without forgetting its past.

"The education of the hand has always been an essential part of life here at Berea College. Working individually and together . . . our students discover and enrich their artistic and problem-solving potential, starting with the most basic raw materials and creating objects of utility, beauty, and expression," he writes in Berea's stunning craft catalog.

Almost 90 percent of first-year students assigned to Student Craft will apply to stay in the following years, joining upper classmates.

"When students see a tangible product at the end of the day, they want to stay involved," Beale told me.

The students make brooms, throw pots, weave blankets, and craft small wooden items like Skittle games and baskets. Some students opt to work with larger wood items and have made dining room chairs for the Kentucky governor's mansion and a long extension table for the Berea president's house. Labor students from other departments conduct market analyses and design the catalog. Their confidence is palatable.

I once marveled at a lovely handwoven yellow baby blanket that Anna Ernberg built and was being sold in the Log House Craft Gallery on campus.

"What would happen if I was a first-year student assigned to weaving but could not make something as nice as this?" I asked the Berea student staffing the counter.

"I don't understand your question," she responded politely.

"What if I could not weave a blanket good enough to sell in the store," I said.

"Oh," she answered, "We'd work with you until you could."

Now eager to inspire students to think creatively, Beale has hired, as a consultant, Stephen Burks, possibly the best-known African American designer working today.

"When the college called, I had never heard of it, and then I was blown away by its history, its diversity, and its crafts," Burks said on a PBS documentary.

Working collaboratively with master craftspeople, Burks and the students have conceived new designs, marketed as the Crafting Diversity collection, that include colorful baskets and handwoven pillows. The college has signed an agreement with Design Within Reach, a modern furnishing company, as the exclusive outlet for this new collection; sales have been steady. In 2021, those items amounted to 20 percent of all craft revenues.

In the spring of 2023, fourteen students, independent of Burks, were listed as designers of record for new items that will be delivered to Design Within Reach. Preliminary orders already represent

23 percent of revenue projections. Design Within Reach asked if it could purchase 100 percent of the weaving products, but Beale and his colleagues decided not to do that.

"It is worth noting," says Beale, "that Design Within Reach buys all the products with no wholesale discount. . . . They pay full retail price and resell the items for the same price, leaving 100 percent of the revenue with Berea."

LABOR BEYOND CRAFTS

In years two through four, students apply for their annual labor assignments from 125 different opportunities, from staffing the front desk at the Boone Tavern Hotel to providing services to the Hispanic Outreach Program and giving tours for potential students.

Chapman Evans ('22) structured a new position within dining services. Unrelated to his major in neuroscience, but wanting to inject more fun on campus, he pitched a new labor assignment under the tutelage of dining services. He introduced karaoke and trivia nights in the dining hall. "I became the Admiral of Entertainment," he said.

Hunter McDaniel ('23) showed similar initiative, which opened up future pursuits for him. A talkative young man with a cheery personality, he grew up in Kingsport, Tennessee, in what he calls "the dirtiest city in the state." When he was three, his parents divorced, both remarried, and both divorced again.

"My father works at Walmart. My mother stayed at home and spent her child support on foolish things. She's not reliable," he says forthrightly.

The Office of Student Life offers day trips on many weekends, and when McDaniel first arrived, he signed up for rock climbing, something he had never done as a kid. He was hooked.

"Poor people don't have the time or the money to enjoy adventure. . . . And most outdoor activities tend to be kind of bro-y, a 'Hey, dude,' kind of thing," says this openly gay young man.

McDaniel majored in health and human performance and, for his labor position, worked in student life, trying to attract a more diverse group for outings. He eventually became student manager of an ever-increasing list of free trips. Along with one other student, he handled all the administrative tasks for the free trips, ran the lottery system for popular events like white water rafting and backpacking, kept the books, and reported all finances to the program's anonymous donor.

For his senior project, McDaniel surveyed what other colleges do for outdoor adventure education, why they chose that approach, and how they implement it, particularly for marginalized communities, and then he structured a possible minor for Berea to consider.

Students on a field trip at Carter Caves. Courtesy of student photographer Ruth Oremus/Berea College.

Based on that work, he applied for and won the prestigious yearlong Watson Fellowship to study nature-based treatments for chronic diseases and mental health issues in Scotland, Japan, Australia, and New Zealand.

Andrea Patton ('24) did not show McDaniel's initiative. She was assigned to housekeeping her first year and stayed with it for another year, even though, by her own admission, she had not made many connections and found it unfulfilling, but she had struggled those first two years and almost dropped out of college. She went quiet when I asked why she thought Berea had accepted her.

"I don't know," she said, "Maybe because I took my ACTs several times."

But slowly I learned that in high school she had volunteered for the Rotary Club and in a local nursing home; she had competed on the high school "college bowl" team, all the while caring for her mother, who is disabled. In her third year at Berea, she applied to the Center for Excellence in Learning Through Service (CELTS), and the advisers suggested she work with the Adopt-a-Grandparent program.

When we spoke, she had just recruited and organized volunteers to work a "senior prom" at a nursing home in Lexington, helping the elderly women with their hair and makeup, serving them drinks, and urging them to dance. She said it was like catering a fancy party.

"Now I have found a purpose," said this young sociology major from central Kentucky.

EVALUATION

In 2021 on the annual survey students must complete, 4 out of 5 students said that their labor assignments helped with their academic progress; 3 out of 5 had work directly related to their majors;

and 4.4 out of 5 said their labor assignments were very important to their overall Berea experience.

The labor supervisors take an annual survey, too. In 2021, the supervisors said 36 percent of the students' work was exceptional, 37 percent exceeded expectations, and 24 percent met expectations. Two percent needed improvement, and 1 percent failed. Those who fail their labor assignments are usually sent to the farm as an alternative assignment.

"But doesn't that insult those who choose to work on the farm?" I asked three students with whom I had dinner one evening at a neighborhood restaurant.

"Oh, no," answered Grayson Collier ('22), a biology major from a family in Whitesburg, Kentucky, that is always taking in foster kids.

"The students sent for disciplinary reasons do the drudge work like weeding the vegetable garden; the rest of us do really interesting things like sticking our hands up a cow's butt," she said laughing. Her animal science class used the farm as a laboratory.

Meanwhile, after Taylor Miles graduated in 2020 in agriculture and natural resources, she went on for a master's degree at the University of Kentucky in science translation and outreach. Now living on a twelve-acre farm outside Berea that she and her husband bought, she runs the University of Kentucky's Estill County extension program for young 4-H members, teaching children "about ecologically sound restorative ag where every choice is environmentally smart." She organizes day camps, afterschool activities, livestock retreats, and weekly activities in agriculture, healthy living, and the expressive arts. She calls them 4-H's Great Commitments.

SERVICE BEYOND LABOR

Some 35 percent of all students at Berea engage in service outside their labor assignments—some of it voluntary and as traditional as tutoring a child, mentoring a teenager, or adopting a grandparent, as Andrea Patton was doing. Some students provide a service as required in a class. To help professors design such interactive courses, CELTS mounts weeklong, interdisciplinary workshops for them.

"Not too long ago many professors resisted the notion of experiential learning, but now they rarely do," says Ashley Cochrane, director of CELTS. Astronomy students have collected the stories Native Americans told about stars to enrich curricula at the local public schools and stargazing nights at the Berea College Forest. Computer science students have designed programs and analyzed data for local community-based organizations; others have provided health education materials in Ghana in partnership with a leading nursing/midwife college; and students in sustainability and environmental studies have conducted energy audits of businesses in eastern Kentucky.

BRUSHY FORK AND BONNER SCHOLARS

As a high school sophomore, Ethan Hamblin from Gays Creek, Kentucky, attended the Brushy Fork Institute at Berea along with scores of other community leaders throughout central Appalachia. Brushy Fork, founded by and funded by Berea, supports grassroots leaders throughout central Appalachia. A strong student and a talented church organist, Hamblin learned at Brushy Fork how to design and launch a website for the distinctive and historic Buckhorn Log Cathedral near his home. During that session, Ethan fell in love with the campus and afterward visited so many times that when he was accepted, an admissions counselor said, "Honey, we were scared you'd burn the place down if we didn't accept you." Hamblin enrolled, majored in Appalachian studies, and became a Bonner Scholar.

Corella Allen Bonner did not go to Berea, but she could have. She had a peripatetic and poor childhood in the coal mining towns of Tennessee, West Virginia, and Kentucky before moving with her mother to Detroit when she was fourteen. She worked her way up from cashier to manager at a Detroit hotel, and then the hotel chain transferred her to New York City, where she was a manager at a famous hotel.

She met Bertram Bonner, an ambitious young man on Wall Street, and they married in 1942. Bertram left Wall Street, entered the competitive and lucrative field of real estate development, and eventually built and sold houses up and down the East Coast. The family became wealthy, and Corella became a pillar of civic life in their hometown of Princeton, New Jersey. One day a doctor's assistant, inquiring about Corella's southern accent, told her about Berea's historic commitment to people like her—poor but talented with an emphasis on learning, labor, and service. Intrigued, the Bonners made a few small gifts to the college, and then in 1990 Corella and Bertram Bonner, a young colleague, and John Stephenson, president of Berea (1984–1994) met and devised a program to help low-income students at Berea connect direct service with policy work and, by doing so, gain valuable lessons in leadership. Now more than forty-five colleges have Bonner Scholars.

Every year, Berea chooses fifteen to twenty new Bonners, who for the next four years will fulfill their labor requirements off campus with organizations that address public needs. They will spend two summers working on specific projects, many abroad, that tackle a pressing public issue, and when they graduate from Berea—and almost 80 percent do—they will join some fifteen thousand Bonner alumni.

Hamblin's first labor assignment as a Bonner Scholar was with Kentuckians for the Commonwealth, organizing students and advocacy trips to Frankfort on equity and mountaintop mining issues. His next labor assignments were back with the Brushy Fork Institute, helping design and implement workshops for other future Appalachian leaders. Hamblin is now the Appalachian program officer for the Mary Reynolds Babcock Foundation in Durham, North Carolina, doing the kind of community work he dreamed of doing as a kid in Gays Creek, Kentucky.

CELTS, the Center for Internships and Career Development, and the Center for International Education maintain an extensive web of volunteer projects, paid summer internships, and international service projects for students to explore. All the centers have students who help their peers navigate various avenues. Not all projects need to be away; Berea will support students financially who work for not-for-profit organizations back in their hometowns for the summer, and the college will support many unpaid internships that relate to a student's major area of study.

The list of possibilities is long, and as Cochrane says, "Berea students are accepted in part because of their demonstrated interest in service to their communities, so it's our job to give them as many opportunities to do that. And maybe along the way we can help them discover new passions."

In 2022, Cochrane submitted a formal proposal to the college that service by students be treated like labor, with evaluations and transcripts.

7

THE KINSHIP OF ALL PEOPLE

To assert the kinship of all people and to provide interracial education with a particular emphasis on racial healing and equity among Blacks and whites as a foundational gateway toward understanding and equality among all peoples of the earth.

F ee called it "impartial love." The Day Law of 1904 highjacked Fee's dream of interracial harmony, but the Fifth Great Commitment reasserted that imperative between Black and white people and "all peoples of the earth." President Roelofs said it well when he wrote in August 2020, "God has made of one blood all peoples of the earth . . . is not only Berea's motto, it is a way of understanding our relationship to humanity. It says no matter what our differences, we have shared kinship."

Berea nurtures shared kinship by building an immersive community that strives to raise personal awareness; foster understanding, not just tolerance; and increase appreciation of the other.

UNDERSTANDING THE KIN IN KINSHIP

Berea's Dee Hill-Zuganelli, an associate professor of family studies and a practicing clinician, begins his class on family relations on how nuclear families shape perceptions and behavior, and set future patterns of conduct or expectations. His students are primarily majors in child and family studies, psychology, or education, but his teaching assistant Dayton Nicholson ('23) believes the course should be mandatory for every student at Berea. "Absolutely," Nicholson said.

On the day I visited, they were reviewing the academic roots and practical uses of genograms, the graphic representations of significant events or actions of individual family members over three or more generations. They had read the definitive paper on genograms by Monica McGoldrick, Randy Gerson, and Sueli Petry.

"Nuclear families provide moral training, spiritual guidance, and cultural connections to rituals and beliefs that help people make sense of what they are 'supposed' to do in life and why things are the way they are," Hill-Zuganelli explained.

The students pored over sample genograms of a hypothetical family with the various symbols that accompanied or connected people with events or behaviors. The permutations were numerous and varied, depending on who had filled in the graph and for what purpose, explained Hill-Zuganelli. Doctors might use medical histories, marriage counselors might use divorce histories, social workers might use mental health conditions or familial violence, and peer counselors might look for substance abuse. Interestingly, Hill-Zuganelli emphasized the possibility and even the desirability to structure a genogram of nonfamily members to assess positive relationships. "Kin has a traditional shape, but we can also choose new families. Sometimes it is wise to do so," he said.

The students, working in small teams, discussed their separate genograms, looking for patterns and hypothesizing about what behaviors those earlier patterns might have produced. The discussions remained general, not specific, but I could tell the students were eager to master the software that would allow them to graph their own families over the upcoming holiday, as assigned.

Nicholson, the teaching assistant, announced with theatrical gusto his availability to help anyone master the software. A child and family studies major with a minor in theater, his complementary interests shone bright that morning.

"You know me," he said to the class with flair, "I'm kind of a mess, but a good mess."

When they had completed their own genograms at home, they might, Hill-Zuganelli said, have more insight into themselves and their respective families, the first step in understanding the concentric rings of kinship, of which kin is the first ring.

One of those concentric circles of kinship emerged one day in Channell Barbour's ('91) office without the benefit of a formal genogram. As former Vice President of Student Life, Barbour knows virtually every student on campus and handles some of the most troublesome situations. Recently, a white boy from eastern Kentucky who hung out with a group of other white guys on campus was heard using offensive and threatening language.

"It was neo-Nazi stuff," explained Barbour. She summoned the student to chat with her, and it soon became clear that he had been bullied at home by his tougher, big brothers. "Then it came out that he had a Black sister. I did not ask him why. Too many Berea kids have complicated family lives with multiple fathers and mothers, but I asked him what he would do if anyone did or said ugly things to his sister. He burst out crying, saying over and over that he loved her. There he was sobbing in my office."

Steps to understanding and sharing kinship can be steep and, as Jessica Klanderud, an American historian and director of the Carter G. Woodson Center for Interracial Education, said, "Poverty makes equals of everyone at Berea until it doesn't. . . . Racism is not personal; it's societal, and sometimes, it's psychological."

BUILDING COMMUNITY BETWEEN THE RACES

In 1950, when the Kentucky legislature amended the Day Law, a grim racial climate still hovered over the land. Berea slowly reintegrated, trying hard to return to Fee's original dream of equality between the races. But it took time for the college to rebuild the trust needed to recruit Black students and staff. By 2021, African American students represented 29 percent of the student body and Hispanics 14 percent.[1] There were 138 full-time faculty members, with 10 percent Black and 5 percent Hispanic; the same ratio existed on the administrative staff. The college knows more work needs to be done on the hiring front, and it knows that integration among students means more than numbers.

The summer of 2021. Courtesy of Crystal Wylie/Berea College.

But just as families relate better if they know how they are connected to and influenced by their kin, kinship cannot flourish without an understanding of the other, too. Channell Barbour said that national political divisions, police shootings, Black Lives Matter protests, and social media have made racial tensions more common on campus than in the recent past. She insists that confronting tension, however difficult, can lessen them.

"Berea is first and foremost an educational institution, and we need to treat racial tension as learning opportunities. Not everyone comes to Berea understanding its values, and we need to teach them. We cannot coddle kids and then also talk about accountability. There's work to be done," said this no-nonsense, fast-talking, and fast-moving administrator.

She tells me about a young white girl from the mountains of Tennessee who continually used the N-word in front of her Black roommate. The Black girl asked her roommate to stop, to no avail, so she went to Dr. Barbour's office and demanded to be moved or threatened to hit the white girl.

"Every time something uncomfortable comes up, our reaction cannot be to just remove the problem," said Barbour, the youngest of seven children who was told by her college counselor that she wasn't college material and should consider cosmetology ("I didn't even know what that was," she said, laughing). "I told the Black girl I would not move her, nor, as some of my colleagues wanted, would I suspend the white girl. Where's the education in *any* of that?"

Instead, Barbour told the Black girl what plan she had and then summoned the white girl to her office. They spoke and Barbour told her she needed to research and write a paper on the history of the N-word and its emotional, political, and social impact on African Americans; she should work with the director of the Black Cultural Center on the paper.

Once the student finished the paper satisfactorily, the college organized one of its periodic Truth Talks, where difficult social and political issues are discussed—everything from tensions between Israel and Palestine to gun rights to the trust between African Americans and Africans. The most popular Truth Talk was "Questions You Want to Ask Another Race." Held late in the afternoon so that many faculty, students, and staff can join, these talks allow participants, if they want, to use interactive technology to remain anonymous with their questions.

At this Truth Talk, as Barbour described it, the white girl from Tennessee joined the director of the Black Cultural Center and a Black student studying African American history on a panel to discuss the N-word. The white girl was not shamed and no one called her out for her previous insults.

"Things settled down and the two girls stayed roommates for a year," said Barbour, smiling. "It might have been a somewhat uneasy truce, but the Black girl will always have a story to tell and, maybe, one day the white girl will hear the N-word and say, 'I once got in trouble for saying that and this is why.'" Barbour paused and then added, "It's hard work, and Berea can be messy."

I asked President Roelofs about this incident, and he said, "We are inclusive at the front end with the expectation that even if you have suffered harm and prejudice in your life, you must welcome those who have harmed you," he replied.

Another powerful example of that perspective comes, again, with Ethan Hamblin ('14), the Bonner Scholar mentioned in the previous chapter. When he was a junior, he was on his way to a party in drag, and he bumped into a young girl, a first-year student, whom he knew from eastern Kentucky.

"She freaked out," said Hamblin. "She cried over and over again and said she had to leave Berea; she couldn't stay. Why? I asked her. You have as much right to be here as I do."

The Campus Christian Center helped, organizing sessions where they could talk it through. The girl stayed and eventually graduated.

KNOWING ONE'S HISTORY AND THE HISTORY OF THE OTHER

Beyond self-awareness and conflict resolution, knowing about the achievements of others can also enhance kinship. Carter G. Woodson (1903) was not Berea's first Black graduate, but he might be the one with the most significant impact nationwide. He was born in December 1875 in New Canton, Virginia, the fourth of nine children. Woodson's father, an illiterate freedman, always approached the front door, not the back door, of a white man's house and imbued his son with self-respect and dignity.

As a child, Carter walked to his uncles' one-room schoolhouse in rural Virginia before he followed his older brother to the booming coal mines of Huntington, West Virginia, some 350 miles due west. He worked in the mines of the New River Gorge and heard stories from other Black miners about the Civil War and Reconstruction. Many years later Woodson wrote, "[There] my interest in penetrating the past of my people deepened."

He eventually went to the one high school for Black students in Huntington and, in 1897, hearing about Berea, traveled 115 miles south to enroll there. By then the debate between Booker T. Washington, president of Tuskegee Institute in Alabama, and W. E. B. Du Bois, a sociologist at Atlanta University, was raging, with each writing articles and shaping curricula that reflected their opinions. Booker T. Washington, although acknowledging the importance of education, believed that without economic independence, Black Americans would never achieve equality; Tuskegee Institute offered teacher training as well as carpentry, brickmaking, and other vocations. W. E. B. Du Bois, a northerner, argued the opposite. He had witnessed Jim Crow's cruelty as a student at Fisk University in Nashville, Tennessee, and then returned to Massachusetts to become the first Black American to get a PhD at Harvard University. He said and debated vigorously that education and civil rights was the way for Black Americans to achieve equality. Black Americans, he stressed, had to show white people that they could achieve at the highest level and, thus, challenge the pervasive view that Black people were inferior.

Although John Fee did not address this debate in his autobiography, he and his colleagues were committed to full equality between the races; it is safe to presume that he fell on the side of W. E. B. Du Bois and, thus, offered a traditional liberal arts education,

"Educating Blacks and whites, men and women was radical, but teaching the liberal arts to Black people was a game changer," said Jessica Klanderud, the director of Berea's Carter Woodson Center.

At Berea, Woodson studied Greek, Roman history, English, geometry, Plato—a classic liberal arts curriculum of the day. He then returned to West Virginia, served as principal of the high school he had attended, and eventually volunteered to teach in the Philippines at an American school. It was 1904. There he discovered that, like Black Americans, Filipinos were not taught about their own history either. When Woodson returned to study at the University of Chicago and then Harvard, one professor said to him, "Black people have no history."[2] But Woodson knew different.

He began to study and document Black history, wanting to "free the mind from the distorted image of the Negro by many a social scientist and a repressive society." He founded, edited, and widely distributed the *Journal of Negro History* to both Black and white people—scholars, civic-minded people, religious leaders; the journal highlighted articles about the achievements of Black Americans, and, by doing so, gave them pride and agency. In 1926, Woodson inaugurated Black History Week, and sixty years later the United States officially declared February Black History Month.[3] In 2011, Berea opened the Carter G. Woodson Center for Interracial Education; it's the first space one sees when entering the Alumni Building. Its library, named for James Hathaway, a freedman who graduated from Berea in 1874 and became president of the Kentucky State University, is replete with books about race in America, the Civil War, Reconstruction, northern migration, and other multicultural issues.

The Day Law of 1904 highjacked Fee's dream of interracial harmony, but the Fifth Great Commitment reasserted that imperative between Black and white people and "all peoples of the earth." Berea tries to facilitate such understanding statewide. The Association for Teaching Black History in Kentucky, led by a Berea graduate, Chaka Cummings ('02), and housed at the Carter G. Woodson Center, works with others to uncover and disseminate stories about accomplished Black Kentuckians in K–12 classes.

"The goal is to really think locally about history across Kentucky and where the lens of Black Kentuckians can be integrated within the tapestry of local history across the commonwealth," said Cummings at the association's inaugural conference in February 2023.

ASSERTING KINSHIP INTERNATIONALLY

Francis S. Hutchins, president of Berea from 1939 to 1967, defined kinship globally. He grew up in Berea, where his father, William J. Hutchins, was president (1920–1939). After college, Francis lived in China for more than fifteen years, setting up exchange programs to enhance cross-cultural understanding and knowledge and marrying the daughter of American missionaries. In 1939, they returned to the States when he succeeded his father and became president of Berea.[4]

Hutchins guided Berea through the final years of the Great Depression, World War II, the end of the Day Law, the rise of the civil rights movement, and the school's growing dedication to cross-cultural understanding. The college began actively to enroll international students and encourage them to share their cultures—food, music, dance, stories, literature—with each other and domestic students.

One day during his tenure, Hutchins was escorting a Pakistani educator, dressed in a colorful silk sari, around the campus. At a distance, the visitor spotted a bald monk, dressed in saffron robes.

"Who is that?" she asked Hutchins with surprise.

"Oh, he's the superintendent of Buddhist education in Cambodia," Hutchins answered. "He's visiting, too."

"Then it is true," she responded. "Eventually everyone comes to Berea."

THE SEEDS OF THE PEACE CORPS

David Kelley ('51) from Lansing, Michigan, attended Berea during Hutchins's tenure. While there, he was chair of the relatively new Students for Democratic Action (SDA), which, in his own words, "sought to build a liberal student movement—a phenomenon never before seen in our society." In June 1951, Berea hosted the fourth annual convention of SDA with attendees from sixty different colleges. They unanimously voted to establish an organization that would recruit young American men and women to work to improve health, education, sanitation, transportation, and production in developing countries around the world. After he graduated, David Kelley established and led a new not-for-profit, the International Development Placement Association (IDPA), which would spearhead the ambitious dream of building shared kinship.

By 1954, the IDPA had a high profile and influential endorsements, including from Eleanor Roosevelt and Hubert Humphrey, the future Vice President of the United States. It had received more than five hundred applications and placed eighteen young men and women in India, Nigeria, Indonesia, and Uganda. Sadly, it was unable to raise enough money to continue and closed, but the dream lived on.

In 1961, John F. Kennedy, the newly elected president of the United States, having heard through his political rival Hubert

Humphrey about the IDPA, announced the beginning of what he called the Peace Corps, based on the exact same principles.

Kelley was asked to go to Washington, DC, and handle recruitment for the new Peace Corps. Soon, excited by the opportunity, he, too, joined, and he and his young family moved to Cameroon in West Africa. There he learned that the traditional arts of Cameroon—woodcarving, basket weaving, and pottery—were disappearing, just like Appalachian crafts, and so Kelley and his Cameroon neighbors established the Bamenda Handicraft Cooperative. Some 1,300 member artisans began to sell their crafts locally, nationally, and internationally.

Today, the Bamenda Handicraft Cooperative still thrives; more than 240,000 Americans have served in the Peace Corps; and every year students from seventy different countries study at Berea, helping build kinship among all the peoples of the earth.

A SHARED KINSHIP WITH TIBETANS

In 1988, Khando Chazotsang visited Berea along with seven other senior Tibetans-in-exile from Dharamshala, India. They came as guests of the US State Department to study marginalized communities and how they maintained their cultural heritages. They visited Mennonites, Amish, Native Americans, and Appalachian communities; the Boone Tavern Hotel in Berea served as home base for their visit to eastern Kentucky.

"At Berea, we saw students making brooms and furniture along with their formal studies. We saw ourselves in those students as we, too, believe in self-sufficiency, cultural preservation, and religious tolerance," Chazotsang said on the telephone from her current home in Utah.

On the third day of their stay, Chazotsang, the only woman on the trip, approached President John Stephenson (1984–1994), identified herself as the niece of the fourteenth Dalai Lama, and asked,

Beacon of Light. Courtesy of student photographer Nay Kaw/Berea College.

point blank, if Berea would give scholarships to Tibetan students. He said it would try.

Six years later, in April 1994, the Dalai Lama, dressed in his traditional maroon and yellow robes with bare arms and beaded prayer bracelets wrapped around his left wrist, arrived at the college.

He spent three days, meeting faculty and the nine Tibetan students then on campus.

"A kind, friendly man . . . with a beaming, nearly perpetual smile and a deep laugh," wrote Howard Wilkinson, a reporter from Cincinnati.

Stephenson, a Presbyterian, took the Dalai Lama, a Buddhist, to visit the gravesite of Thomas Merton, a Catholic, who is buried at the Abbey of Gethsemani about eighty miles west of Berea. On his last day at Berea, with the governor of Kentucky present, the Dalai Lama preached, magnifying the promise of shared kinship: "Peace will come to the world when humankind looks within itself, each one of us, to the goodness and gentleness inside."

In 2022, three Tibetan students studied at Berea. The most recent arrival, a young woman, left Tibet for India when she was only seven with her little sister. They walked across the mountains in a small group her parents trusted. When we met, she had not seen her parents for fourteen years and remains circumspect in letters back to Tibet. Studying biology, she fulfills her labor assignment on the Berea farm, and joins 135 young people on campus from Brazil to Burundi, Uganda to Uzbekistan.

THE PROCESS

Potential foreign students hear about Berea through US consulates, Google, word of mouth, and Peace Corps volunteers. Yryskeldi Emilbek uulu ('22), known as Ari on campus, grew up in the central Asian nation of Tajikistan. His widowed mother lost her restaurant in the capital city when the Soviets ruled and now lives on a subsistence farm in the countryside. Ari heard about Berea through his sister, who now works in women's affairs of the Tajikistan government.

Berea charges no application fee for foreign applicants, and the Admissions Office receives about three thousand international applications annually. Like their US counterparts, the applicants must show academic promise and a commitment to service, but unlike most American colleges, which seek foreign students who can pay the full cost, Berea admits only low-income students.[5] To that end, applicants must submit financial reports, including third-party verification of their poverty. The Admissions Office rejects almost half of the applicants outright based on the absence of apparent financial need.[6]

Offering no English language courses for foreign students, the college requires proof of English proficiency, and applicants may submit scores from one of several tests, including the Test of English as a Foreign Language, better known as TOEFL, and a Duolingo test. Once accepted, every international student receives free tuition for four years, work assignments, and one round-trip airline ticket home.

THE CENTER FOR INTERNATIONAL EDUCATION

Ari arrived in the summer of 2018 and immediately took the mandatory intensive orientation class with the other first-year international students—including information on proper male/female relationships—that the Center for International Education (CIE) structures.

CIE, led by Dr. Richard Cahill, a Middle East expert fluent in Arabic, focuses on both domestic students who want to study abroad for a summer, a winter, or an entire semester and all the international students. The office handles everything from immigration complexities to relationships with partner organizations around the world to the recruitment of professors and students for study trips. The CIE takes the Fifth Great Commitment as its guiding principle: help all students meet and appreciate a wide swath of cultures and perspectives, seek the similarities, and celebrate the differences.

Cahill, his three staff members, and eleven labor students host, for instance, Think Globally, It's Friday (TGIF). International students and domestic students who have studied abroad prepare meals (with help from the CIE staff) from their respective nations. TGIF has become the most popular weekly event at the college, drawing 160 students at each.

Every year (except the COVID-19 years), the CIE also focuses its Mundo Monthly events on one region, inviting outside experts, Fulbright Scholars, and dance troupes for lectures or performances and, of course, food. In October 2019 (before COVID-19 came), the focus was on Latin America. The speaker (an old friend of Cahill's) was a longtime community organizer, youth coordinator, high school teacher, and lawyer in Medellín, notably in Comuna 13, a community that was ground-zero for Pablo Escobar and his narco-violence/ urban warfare and that later made a remarkable rebirth. I did not get to hear him, but others report the students were glued to his stories. In 2023, Mundo Monthly focused on the Middle East.

I attended several CIE events and invariably learned something new or heard someone impressive—and ate good food—and, as an outsider looking in, I kept reminding myself that most of the students in that auditorium had never traveled outside their counties, states, or, in some cases, their refugee camps until they came to Berea. Now they can travel, or as one student said to Richard Cahill, "I felt as if I visited four continents during my four years at Berea just by going to Mundo Monthlys."

One Saturday afternoon, Ari and I had our own little CIE event. We drove together into the knobs east of the college. I wanted to see the town of Beattyville, recently heralded by CNN for its rejuvenation, and Ari wanted to see the vegetation in the mountains as he worked on a paper about the correlation between soil erosion, acidity, and plant communities. I also needed a navigator. We wandered around a Family Dollar Store in McKee, Kentucky, checking items and their prices, ate lunch at the Bobcat Dairy Bar outside Beattyville, and drove in vain around the town but never found the artists' space that CNN had touted on air. But Ari enjoyed his first American milkshake and together we made it back to campus.

BUILDING UNDERSTANDING FOR DREAMERS

Closer to home, in 2008 the state of Georgia passed a law that prohibits any DACA (Deferred Action for Children Arrivals) recipient living in the state from attending a state college or university. In disgusted response, a small group of professors, first at the university in Athens, Georgia, and later in Atlanta, offered free college preparatory classes for DACA high school students on Sunday afternoons.

Freedom University grew, and in 2017 Berea raised its hand and said it would accept Dreamers from Freedom University. Six enrolled. DACA students are not eligible for Pell grants or most state-based aid programs, so Berea raises the money privately for them.

The DACA issue, however, remains loaded as political debates about immigration rage and DACA students become political ping-pong balls. Although Immigration and Customs Enforcement has never come to campus or asked for the university's cooperation, the continuing uncertainty about immigration policy churns up waves of fear and anxiety among some students, but Berea wraps them with the kind of emotional support their close kin might.

BUILDING COMMUNITY WITH INDIVIDUALITY

Assimilation with individuality is how Vice President for Alumni, Communications and Philanthropy Chad Berry describes what Berea tries to do with all its students. Poverty and labor are the equalizers among all Berea students, and sports can help some kids differentiate themselves. A Division III college and member of the NCAA, Berea has eight competitive teams for both men and women, including basketball, soccer, women's volleyball, and a successful long-distance running team. Every student must also pass a swim test before graduation—a rule in place since the gym was built in 1928 with the first college pool in the state. Kevin Moreno

Mountain Day. Courtesy of student photographer Anh Ngo/ Berea College.

Tapia, a '22 Dreamer, and Ari from Tajikistan lifted weights together most days and took the swimming exam together.

Music and dance are also paths to individuality and community. Some 67 percent of all Berea students participate in ten different performing music groups and nine different dance groups. They range from a jazz band to Southeast Asian dancers. These groups, open to all, highlight individual talents, recognize budding interests, and build shared experiences between individuals of different backgrounds.[7]

On Mountain Day in mid-October, a tradition that began in 1875, the college cancels all classes, and after a voluntary sunrise hike up the Pinnacles, one of many hiking trails that crisscross the Berea Forest, students perform for one another in the small amphitheater tucked into the woods, with the acts including bluegrass, Afro-Latin, and mariachi band music as well as Middle Eastern, Appalachian, and Latino dance.

The diversity among the students, their shared interests, and their obvious appreciation for one another proves that diversity in all its variations enriches education and community strengthens kinship. Take note, Supreme Court.

EMBEDDING KINSHIP

As a little boy, biracial Alex Gibson ('08) moved from Cincinnati to Jackson County, Kentucky, and suffered racist slurs constantly in his all-white rural community. He never felt as if he belonged and carried anger with him.

"Being multiracial means your story is often one of struggle against the tides of an unyielding majority, not to mention the struggles within yourself," Gibson said.

His mother was fired from her nursing job and then disabled in a car accident; his father was in prison and his older brother was schizophrenic, addicted to drugs. By the time Alex was sixteen, both his parents had died and Alex was alone. That summer, he visited Berea on an Upward Bound trip.

"A male nursing student was my tour guide—I never knew Black men could be nurses before then—and as we walked, a white Appalachian kid, you know, the kind with a long straggly beard, was shooting down Chestnut Street on a skateboard in a skirt, and I knew Berea was the place for me. I knew I could be me there."

The Upward Bound rep at Berea urged Gibson to apply to the Piney Woods School in Mississippi, a boarding school, and then to consider Berea. He did both and returned to Berea and studied philosophy. He eventually served as student representative to the board of directors and student government president, brought Oxfam to campus as a Bonner Scholar, and worked in a hacienda every summer in Mexico. There he met indigenous people who did not speak English, lived off the land with only poor roads leading to market, sent their children to schools even worse than the roads, and hated the government—not unlike parts of eastern Kentucky where Alex had grown up. He said of the experience, "Mexico helped me put Appalachia into context, and it took much of that anger and simplistic view of racism as simply between Black and white away. It's about power and threat. Berea helped me focus on shared experiences."

When Gibson graduated from Berea in 2008 with a B.A. in philosophy, he won the prestigious Watson Fellowship, given to students annually, chosen from only forty-one colleges nationwide. With its financial support, Gibson traveled for a year to Venezuela, Vietnam, India, and South Africa.

"I wanted to hear the stories of people who, too often, like myself, live their lives in the shadows of trying to find light," he said. He eventually wrote *They Call Us Dust Children: An Exploration of Biracial Identity*.

Then Gibson applied to and was accepted into the University of Pennsylvania Law School, and he credits board members at Berea for advancing his candidacy.

"All good things in my life are rooted in Berea," he said simply.

He studied constitutional law in England and Thailand, graduated, clerked for a federal judge, and then worked as a corporate lawyer, finding himself climbing the same ladder as his privileged classmates at Penn—until he stepped off.

At Berea, he had seen films about Appalachia, produced at Appalshop, the nationally known, community-based, multifaceted arts organization in Whitesburg, Kentucky. He applied to be its new executive director, got the position, and moved—with his wife, a Berea graduate from Kansas—to the mountains. Since 2014, Gibson has reenergized and rebuilt this unique place in the heart of eastern Kentucky. He has guided its radio station and theater, hosted music festivals, executive produced documentary films and plays, trained young people, and collected oral histories—all for, by, and about the Black, white, Latino, and biracial people of eastern Kentucky.

"Identity comes from stories, and at Appalshop, we collect them in all different forms to help shape identity and deflect stereotypes," he explained, sitting outside the two-story wooden Appalshop on a warm July day as his colleagues prepared the stage for an event that night. "Berea showed me that."

Appalshop was flooded when Hurricane Ian swept through eastern Kentucky in September 2022, and now Gibson has, perforce, become a preservationist, rebuilding its archives, its spaces, its equipment, its morale, and its significance to the area.

8

A DEMOCRATIC COMMUNITY

To create a democratic learning community dedicated to gender equality.

Vice President of Alumni, Communications and Philanthropy Berry said Berea has never been "explicitly political . . . it's hard to transform writ large . . . we have a grassroots perspective like John Fee did . . . if we can produce a 'beloved community' here, then our students will do the same when they leave." Every student with whom I spoke agrees.

"Students might be political, but the college itself is apolitical," said Tongtu Zechar ('22), the previously mentioned studio arts major.

"The college does a pretty good job attracting kids who want to make change, but that's not always political change," said Connor Courtney ('23), a political science major and former president of the Student Government Association, reminding me, wisely, that democracy is not necessarily synonymous with political action.

But over time, many politicians have paid homage to Berea's unique history and purposeful mission. In 1908, Theodore Roosevelt congratulated Andrew Carnegie for his $200,000 gift to Berea, writing, "I doubt if you ever gave a like sum of money where the good will be more real or more far reaching than this."

The same year, Woodrow Wilson spoke at Pine Mountain Settlement School in eastern Kentucky, saying, "Every place of education amongst our free people is still a place of schooling, where passion may be cooled, prejudice enlightened, effort steadied, purpose given vision ... American colleges share with Berea this sacred function of enlightenment, and there ought to be universal comradeship with her."

In 1933, Herbert Hoover and his wife chose a Berea graduate to run a mountain school in their summertime community of North Carolina; First Lady Jackie Kennedy invited the Berea Country Dancers to perform at the White House; President George Bush gave the college a Points of Light Award; and in 2004, some fifty-four Berea students traveled with faculty and administrators to witness the inauguration of President Barack Obama. But no involvement in electoral politics has been more deeply embedded in Berea's shared story than its active participation in the struggle for voting rights in Alabama in 1965.

BEREA IN ALABAMA

On Sunday, March 7, 1965, six hundred nonviolent activists gathered in Selma to march to Montgomery to protest the killing of a young Black man by police. Governor George Wallace told the state troopers to stop the protest "anyway they could." Dozens of state troopers and sheriff's deputies—some on horseback, some with gas masks, and all with billy clubs, whips, or rubber tubes—attacked the protesters. White spectators cheered. The cops sprayed tear gas and beat women, children, and men; one policeman cracked the skull of young John Lewis, leader of the Student Nonviolent Coordinating Committee, future seventeen-term US congressman, and recipient of an honorary degree from Berea.

That night some 50 million viewers, including Black and white students at Berea, were watching a much-heralded movie about Nazi Germany when ABC News broke in with vivid and horrifying footage of the brutal violence in Selma. The next day, four defiant Berea students—three white and one Black—left campus with a

sympathetic staff person in his tiny Volkswagen bug to drive almost five hundred miles to join a quickly organized second march in Selma. The Bereans made it, but tensions were high and danger palatable. Martin Luther King Jr., who had come from Montgomery, halted the unauthorized march, and that night a white rabbi from Boston was beaten to death by white racists outside a Selma café. In response, Martin Luther King Jr. called for a massive march on March 21, 1965.

Many Black and white students were eager to go, but the formal involvement of the college became contentious. Fearful of more violence, President Francis Hutchins said no, the college would not pay the $750 needed for the bus, and no, the faculty could not cancel classes, and, yes, students would need permission from their parents or guardians to travel to Montgomery. Angry and disappointed, the students, including the original five, turned to the Student Government Association (SGA) for help. That debate was combative, too.

"The people of Alabama only know the knife, the rope, and the gun. . . . I believe the college's refusal to lend us the bus should make us stop and think," said one student during the heated debates. His and other voices won the day, and the SGA voted forty-three to fourteen against sanctioning the march.

Then, with local members of the Ku Klux Klan (KKK) standing nearby, dressed in their threatening white sheets, the insistent students marched to the red brick president's house on Chestnut Street, accusing Hutchins of turning his back on the activist roots of the college and its commitment to social justice. With rumors swirling of white people in Birmingham stockpiling weapons in anticipation of the march, President Hutchins stood firm.

But the next morning when the bus—paid for by six faculty members and three local clergy members—prepared to head out, President Hutchins was there. He lent his own car. It would be one of four "buddy cars," as they were called, driven by white men that would surround the students' bus. With a prayer, Hutchins sent fifty-eight Bereans off on the five hundred-mile journey.

They drove all day into the night, often led in song by music major Ann Beard Grundy ('68). She had grown up in Birmingham, Alabama, where her father had been minister at the historic Sixteenth Street Baptist Church, which she describes in a lively and informative oral history as the "la-di-da" church for Black professionals.[1] Her father died a few years before the horrific bombing that killed four little girls, whom, Grundy points out, "are never remembered by name." Carrying *The Autobiography of Malcolm X* on the bus, Grundy later admitted she was both scared and enraged, even as she sang.[2]

The group arrived in Montgomery too late to hear the concert that singer/activist Harry Belafonte had arranged. Standing on a makeshift stage of wooden coffins, Sammy Davis Jr., Nina Simone, Bob Dylan, Joan Baez, Tony Bennett, and others entertained—and pumped up—the people who had flocked into Montgomery. Along with hundreds of others, the Bereans slept that night on the muddy ground and, the next day, joined twenty-five thousand people who had answered King's call.

Protected by US marshals and the National Guard, the demonstrators marched through Montgomery. The Bereans, clustered in the middle of the huge crowd, carried American flags and a large white banner with Berea's motto, God has made of one blood all peoples of the earth. They saw "radiant faces in Black neighborhoods and hatred on white faces," writes Dwayne Mack, an American historian at Berea, who now directs its diversity, equity, and inclusion work. The march ended at the Alabama State Capitol, where Governor George Wallace was nowhere to be seen. On a dais sat Rosa Parks and John Lewis, and the Reverend Martin Luther King Jr. gave a rousing speech, addressing his compatriots' impatience; "How long? Not long, because no lie can live forever. How long?

Not long, because you shall reap what you sow. . . . How long? Not long, because the arc of the moral universe is long, but it bends toward justice."[3]

The jubilant Bereans left Montgomery at nine o'clock that night, stopping at the home of a Black freshman in Collinsville, Alabama, whose mother served fried chicken to every person on the bus. Then they continued their long ride back to Berea, learning the next morning that four KKK thugs had shot and killed Viola Liuzzo, a white volunteer from Detroit. Four months later, President Lyndon Johnson signed the landmark Voting Rights Act of 1965, outlawing barriers to voting.

Today, Berea has a different policy, advanced by students, about students' participation in demonstrations. If three adults from the college accompany a group, the college will supply a bus and pay for motel rooms for the protesters. Students have gone to Frankfort, Kentucky, to lobby for gay rights, to Washington, DC, to protest mountaintop removal, to New York for the Occupy Wall Street demonstrations, and to Ferguson, Missouri, to stand in solidarity with protesters after the death of Michael Brown. Furthermore, after the murder of George Floyd when some local people taunted Black students and their white supporters, the college publicly declared its support for Black Lives Matter with a college-wide march and a clear statement from President Roelofs publicly that day. "We pray that the winds of change blowing throughout the nation move us further along Dr. King's arc of the moral universe toward justice. . . . The fight for a world shaped by the power of love over hate, human dignity and equality, and peace with justice is far from over. The names of George Floyd and Breonna Taylor, among too many others, should forever reside in our conscience as we move forward. Perhaps 50 years from now, but preferably much sooner, we won't have to remind society again that, indeed, Black lives matter."

VOTER REGISTRATION AND PARTICIPATION BY STUDENTS

Emphasizing civic involvement on college campuses is not a new priority. President Harry Truman famously declared that the "first and most essential charge upon higher education is that all levels and in all its fields of specialization, it shall be the carrier of democratic values, ideals, and processes."

Although civic activity on campuses waxes and wanes with the times, recently, given political events and greater polarization, pressure has grown dramatically for colleges to shore up students' understanding of—and dedication to—democratic values in a more systematic and enduring way. Berea, like scores of other colleges and universities, launched a robust voter registration and get-out-the-vote drive among its students.

A faculty, staff, and student committee first identified three major obstacles to voting by students: The campus lies in *four* different voting precincts, confusing students about how to register and where to vote, as their polling place changes whenever they change dormitories; low-income people vote at a lower rate than others—multiple jobs, no transportation, distrust, and disillusionment all play a part—so, many students come to Berea without a familial tradition of voting and need encouragement to do so; and, finally, Berea lies in a deep red county of a red state, and many locals intimidate students voting in the town of Berea. Conversely, Berea's students do not necessarily believe local candidates will have their interests at heart.

The committee launched registration activities, get-out-the-vote initiatives, buddy programs, and research protocols. In 2020, Berea's registration rate was 84 percent, with 67 percent voting. Although slightly lower than the national average, reports Tufts University's Institute on Democracy and Higher Education, the trend is heading in the right direction.[4]

In October 2022, the SGA sponsored a local candidate forum and drew the mayor, five of the eleven candidates for the city council, and candidates for the school board. Students asked questions about broadband and public safety, and together they discussed the need for a space open for both locals and students to break down some of the distance between them.

STUDENT VOICES ON CAMPUS

Berea, like other institutions, invites and encourages student participation in shaping many policies and practices of the college. Student voices and their votes on campus issues give real-life and real-time examples of democratic participation. Berea students serve (without a vote) on administrative committees and even helped shape the recent presidential search process. They organize much of the social life on campus and have lobbied successfully to change policies on dormitory rules, cafeteria practices, and even those guidelines for participation at protests. With student resident advisers and chaplains, students set rules for individual dormitories and serve on judicial committees that mete out consequences for some low-level infractions, taking hits for difficult and controversial decisions.

Tristan Tillery ('24), a premed student turned history major from southern Ohio, has been a resident adviser twice. "The first year was easy and pleasant, but this year has between harder. I've negotiated and enforced a no-contact rule between two people who live across the hall from one another. It was a romantic misunderstanding that got out of control. I am learning a lot, but it's rough."

The SGA has twenty-seven members, who satisfy their labor requirements with their service; the elected student body president appoints them. They meet monthly as a group, loosely following Robert's Rules of Order, setting their own agenda, and doing their work in committees. In 2022, Connor Courtney, SGA president, described one committee that reviewed labor procedures for first-year students including the possibility of recommending that they be able to choose their first-year labor placements and to work before

6:00 a.m. in the morning, if desired. Another committee grappled with the policy on student cars—those who can have them and those who can't. The SGA also recommended new rules on drug and alcohol abuse.

"Berea doesn't have a big drug and alcohol problem, but the SGA set up listening tables, and we kept hearing complaints about too many harsh rules. We are going to suggest that Berea have a medical amnesty policy," Courtney explained. "If a student has a substance abuse problem and tells a college official, the student will get help, not punishment."

DEMOCRACY IN THE CLASSROOMS

David Scobey, a nationally recognized proponent of colleges' role in the strengthening of democracy, defines democratic values as a concern for the common good, meaningful and respectful debate, free speech and free assembly, just and fair decision-making, and equal treatment of all. He acknowledges that much is happening with electoral encouragement and community service on campuses nationwide and cites the Bonner Scholars as leaders.

But he maintains that "strengthening democratic values has not yet become a core value . . . success in preparing students for active participation is piecemeal." It must happen, too, he believes, in the classroom. Contrary to what some might believe, Scobey said, "Democratic values are not divided by politics: many religious schools stress community service, evangelical Christians become environmental activists, and many conservative intellectuals support the study of history, debate, and reasoning."

Project Pericles, a growing consortium of four-year liberal arts colleges, embeds democratic values into courses on their campuses. President Lyle Roelofs chaired its Presidents' Council, and Ashley Cochrane, director of Berea's Center for Excellence in Learning through Service, oversees both the Bonner Scholars and Project Pericles on campus.

Named for the father of Greek democracy, Project Pericles trains faculty to develop civic education curricula in a wide range of disciplines through hands-on activities. At Berea, students studying communications analyzed theories of effective communication and the influence of media on public policy issues, and then designed and implemented a media strategy for the passage of a public health initiative. In an education class, Berea students analyzed the data on higher education loans and student debt, and then conceived, planned, and hosted a summit on the issue. In another education course, a professor teaches contemplative pedagogy and how it can be used to address racism in K–12 classes.

SERVICE LEARNING AND CIVIC ENGAGEMENT

One-third of all Berea students participate in community service or service-learning projects that match academic inquiry with volunteer work. Although some academic researchers question whether community service deepens an understanding of civic responsibility and action, Cochrane believes that "when volunteer work addresses a community need, like poverty or climate change, it embraces the common good and helps develop an appreciation of different solutions to problems, which are both core democratic values."

One ongoing campus-wide focus at Berea has been hunger and health. One-sixth of Kentuckians do not have enough to eat on a regular basis; they are food insecure. In response, Bereans run food drives, throw and sell ceramic bowls to raise funds for food banks, and mount public education campaigns on issues like the high rate of diabetes in eastern Kentucky. Some students then take courses that analyze the many complicated reasons for hunger: They evaluate data, explore the impact of low wages, review food stamp programs, assess nutritional education programs, analyze the economics of food deserts, and examine complex agricultural and transportation challenges. Most of them do this having experienced hunger themselves. Alex Gibson ('08), a former SGA president, said, point-blank, that he had never had three meals a day until he got to Berea.

CELTS director Cochrane said, "Ultimately our goal is to have every student graduate from Berea knowing that there are many ways to address problems in your community: advocacy, analysis, policy jobs, volunteering, protesting, voting."

Ben Timby ('13) is a case in point. A tall, bearded agriculture and natural resources major from Colorado, he spent one summer living at a Mexican orphanage, designing and building a sustainable irrigation system in its orchard as he practiced Spanish. Berea's Center for International Education supported that trip with funds earmarked for service learning. Then, back at Berea, Timby and his colleagues, working with a faculty member, increased the percentage of college-grown food in the cafeteria by expanding the farm's horticulture fields, adding new water lines, extending the growing season by erecting hoop houses, and improving the stormwater runoff infrastructure.

Timby was neither a Bonner Scholar nor a Pericles participant, but he exemplifies the inextricable link between direct action, policy changes, and civic engagement as well as Berea's efforts to help students connect them. Timby loves Berea, thanks Berea, but still harbors disappointment that the Berea Board refuses to divest entirely from its oil and gas investments. He worked on that issue as a student. Today, he lives in Sitka, Alaska, where he has been active in sustainable, commercial fishing, including the conservation of herring. In classic Berea style, he describes herring as "a harvest of vital cultural and nutritional value to all Alaskans, particularly the tribes which have been harvesting them for thousands of years."

9

A SUPPORTIVE AND
SUSTAINABLE CAMPUS

To maintain a residential campus that encourages in all community members a way of life characterized by mindful and sustainable living, health and wellness, zest for learning, high personal standards, and a concern for the welfare of others.

Berea is strictly a residential college. Students live in fifteen dormitories of various types, including four gender-inclusive ones. Nontraditional students—primarily single mothers—live in Ecovillage, a green apartment complex adjacent to campus. With no sororities, fraternities, or eating clubs, everyone (except residents of Ecovillage) eats together most of the time in the Alumni Building. They enter—three times a day—and go downstairs to the large, airy cafeteria with many stations. Their classmates are behind the counters or in the kitchen, working alongside Sodexo, the large French-based food company that manages the operations.

Students have access to online daily menus and nutritional information, but not surprisingly, they are not always happy. Student advocates from the dining reform movement push for improvements: more choice, less overcooked food, less undercooked food; more vegan options, more vegetarian options. But as Thena Badger ('23) said succinctly, "There are good days, and there are bad days."

The Kentucky Department of Agriculture, on the other hand, celebrated the college with a Lifetime Achievement Award in 2021 for sourcing most of its fresh vegetables, meat, and eggs from farms within fifty miles of the college.

"There's a 30 to 40 percent upcharge to buy local or organic products," explained Derrick Singleton, Vice President for Operations and Sustainability. "The Berea farm helps us financially and helps us meet our sustainability commitment." So does the Berea College Forest.

A SUSTAINABLY MANAGED FOREST

Berea owns nine thousand-plus acres of forest that stretches to and sometimes over the solitary, cone-shaped knobs that signal the start of the Appalachian Mountains. Crisscrossed by hiking trails, the forest, one of the largest private forests in the state, supplies the college and the town of Berea with all the water both need from four reservoirs. A new visitors and educational center welcomes scores of hikers on the weekends, visitors to the annual crafts festival in July, and offers a range of workshops, including stargazing and horse logging.

With a small staff, Clint Patterson, Berea's forester, manages the forest sustainably, balancing the economic needs of the college (and society) with the ecological health of the area. A loquacious guy with a floppy cotton hat, Patterson was a kid in southern Illinois when his grandmother showed him the remains of a small playground of ladders, jungle gyms, and play huts grafted together from sycamore trees.

"The tree ladder had some rungs missing and the playhouse had grown shut, but it fascinated me. I tried doing the same with paraffin wax and a pocketknife, but it did not work out so well," he said. "Sugar maples were not a good choice." Now he knows all about sugar maples and sustainable forests.

You will never see bulldozers and stump grinders in the Berea Forest tearing down trees and ripping up the earth, destroying the fragile ecosystem that trees, plants, and animals share. Patterson, his staff, and labor students cut the weak trees first, practicing directional felling so no healthy trees are harmed; they monitor and manage invasive species and propagate native trees, like the American chestnut tree. They do prescribed burning to protect the trees, the watershed, and wildlife, and in a return to the past to protect the future, they utilize Suffolk Punch workhorses to harvest trees.

HORSE LOGGING

John Henry Hite III ('19), a student, was with Mindy, a Suffolk Punch foal, when she was born three weeks early on campus during an unseasonably stormy night in June 2018. "Maybe we just counted wrong," said Hite, referring to Mindy's projected birth date.

Unlike other workhorse breeds, Suffolk Punches, bred in sixteenth-century England as agricultural animals, have not been damaged by entering pulling competitions; short and stocky with good feet and gentle souls, they have a low center of gravity, which gives them more energy for heavy-duty jobs. Suffolk Punches and mules both are perfect for pulling felled trees from forests, but prematurely born horses often suffer poor musculoskeletal development, which for a future workhorse like Mindy would be disastrous.

"She was in bad shape, but the vet showed me how to save her," Hite explained modestly. Mindy recovered, and Hite later joined the world of horse loggers as a full-time employee of the college. Born in Homosassa, Florida, an old fishing village on the Gulf of Mexico coast, Hite worked in his father's small barbecue restaurant and remembers "washing dishes as soon as I could see the top of the counter."

The family moved to southeastern Kentucky, and when Hite was a high school junior, he moved to the tiny, rural town of Liberty, Kentucky, about fifty miles southwest of Berea, to live with his grandfather, a mechanic, and his grandmother, a manager at Kmart.

I asked him how he thinks he got into Berea, pleading with him not to be modest like so many of his fellow students.

"Everything about me getting into Berea is modest. I was an average student in high school. I got Bs and Cs with the occasional A. My ACT score was a twenty-one, which is average or low. I didn't have any extracurricular or community service. I come from a very low-income family with seven children, so I stayed home and helped take care of my siblings, and when I wasn't doing that, I worked a job to contribute to the household. I went to five different high schools and never stayed anywhere long enough to get very established . . . [but] my Berea interview lasted much longer than the average interview . . . so [maybe] I got in because I was determined to do better in life, and my interviewer could tell that. Berea exists for people like me . . . people with potential but no opportunity."

His first labor assignment at Berea was in the dining hall, but in Year Two, he applied to work in the forest, decided to major in agriculture and natural resources, and returned each successive year to the forest for his labor assignments. There he learned to wield a chain saw, manage prescribed burns, and care for Suffolk Punches.

Hite was there in 2018 when the college hosted its first free weeklong demonstration of restorative forestry and horse logging. Some three hundred people came, including Wendell Berry, the Kentucky environmentalist and poet and essayist; scores of horse and mule loggers; Jason Rutledge, the grand old man of animal logging; and owners of small forests from up and down the East Coast.

Many holders of private forests in Kentucky and elsewhere earn money by selling their timber periodically.[1] If they hire commercial outfits to cut the timber, those companies will carve wide paths to accommodate bulldozers that damage young trees and render future harvests worthless. So, for owners of small forests who care about the natural beauty of the forests and the environment as well as some future income, horse or mule logging makes good sense.

A horse logger, two students, and Suffolk Punches harvesting wood in Berea Forest. Courtesy of Justin Skeens.

"Animal-powered tree removal . . . allows for economically and ecologically sustainable timber harvesting over the life of the forest," said Rutledge. "If you log with horses, you can't tell they've been in the forest, but if you use a skidder the damage lasts 100 years."

Eric Hicks, a plant manager for an automotive parts factory in northern Tennessee, attended the workshop, bringing with him a mule he had raised and hoped to use to harvest timber. Like others, if hired, Hicks will set his fee by the quality of the timber, the ease of access, and then a percentage of the timber sold.

"We worked in that Berea Forest from dawn until dark," Hicks said on the phone. "If we all did what we learned that week, our forests would thrive. Why, just today a local farmer called me and said he wanted to harvest some timber from his thirty-five-acre forest. He didn't want any tractors or logging roads to kill his young trees and asked if I could help. Sure can. Yup, there sure is a need."

Patterson knows that Berea could help address that need and, by doing so, increase the health of the Berea Forest and maybe others, so in 2019 he offered Hite the job of managing the horse logging program.

"I asked myself four things before I accepted," Hite said to me. "What job will support me and give me skills I can always use, no matter what happens in my life. What job leaves the world a better place, and how can I best help my grandparents." Hite took the job.

Now he lives in a college-owned old white clapboard farmhouse near the brand-new red horse barn that sits on a knoll that abuts the Berea Forest. Hite tends and drives four Suffolk Punches and trains other would-be animal loggers to do the same. He has a skill that will last forever and makes the world a better place, and he sees his grandparents weekly and talks to them daily. Hite also returns to Homosassa as often as he can to dive for scallops.

THE HISTORY OF THE BEREA FOREST

Sustainable forestry in Kentucky has its roots in Kansas. At the end of the nineteenth century, the Kansas State College, the first land grant university in the nation, was rocked by debates about its curriculum. "We are not here to make men farmers, but rather farmers men," its president wrote. Frustrated, he soon thereafter moved to Berea, where his brother, E. Henry Fairchild, the first president of Berea College, lived. A few years later, in 1897, President William Frost hired Silas C. Mason, a broad-minded horticultural professor from Kansas State, to manage the farm and teach forestry.

Mason, born in Vermont and raised in Kansas, received both his undergraduate and graduate degrees at Kansas State before traveling to Europe to see how forestry was done there. He returned to Kansas to teach and joined a loose network of people—three in particular—who were also thinking about trees and society.

J. Sterling Morton, a newspaper editor in Nebraska, launched the first annual Arbor Day with the planting of 1 million trees, and by 1884 Arbor Day had gone national. John Muir from Wisconsin fell in love with the majestic redwoods of California and the unique beauty of the Sierra Nevadas and, in 1892, established the Sierra Club to fight for the preservation of spectacular land; and Gifford Pinchot from Connecticut transformed George Vanderbilt's four thousand-acre private forest in North Carolina into a profitable center of lumber production, even as he maintained its ecological stability. Silas Mason would do the same for denigrated woods in poor Kentucky.

But to teach forestry, Berea needed a forest. For years, people living in the steep hollows along the streams of eastern Kentucky felled trees for their houses, barns, and fuel.[2] They clear-cut white oak and poplar trees to plant rows of tobacco and corn, and they floated logs down rivers to sawmills to supplement their paltry incomes. The wounded trees covering the knobs near Berea were sickly and the land destroyed, needing rejuvenation. Within a year of his arrival and with his own money, Mason bought about two hundred acres of depleted woodlands near the school to start the Berea Forest, and on a fundraising trip up north, President Frost met Sarah Bryant Fay.

Fay's father had made a fortune in Savannah, Georgia, shipping southern cotton, picked by enslaved laborers, to the textile mills of New England. Fay was a slave owner, too, and right before the Civil War he left Georgia for good and moved back to Massachusetts. After his death, the self-effacing Sarah, a forty-two-year-old unmarried woman, inherited the family's elegant townhouse and her father's many charitable interests, most of which were woodlands. Frost told Fay about Mason's dream of a forest that would be a living laboratory for talented but impoverished Black and white Appalachian students, a place for their labor assignments and a source of wood for the school.

"I have had a great wish to make such holdings a memorial to my father who was such a tree lover and from which I definitely inherited my taste, but always comes the dread of publicity," Fay said to Frost.

It is unclear if her desire for anonymity was grounded in shame about the money's source or her shyness; however, Frost nonetheless promised her privacy, and she began to donate money to enlarge Berea's Forest. She continued to do so until her "teapot ran dry" in 1915, when the Berea Forest was then 5,500 acres.

With new funds on hand, Mason explored Moonshine Hollow and Cow Bell, Indian Fort, and Big Hill, and miles and miles of other knobs just east of the Berea ridge. He bought overgrazed, overfarmed, and overcut former woodlands for about a dollar an acre. He bought one large parcel of 650 acres for $700 from the daughters of Spicy White, a formerly enslaved woman who had been freed in 1840, and her husband, Richmond Baxter, also emancipated.

"It comes full circle, doesn't it?" Sharyn Mitchell, the former archivist in the special collections at the college, said to me, smiling; Spicy White was her great-great-grandmother.

As Mason walked the forest floor, he noted the trees' conditions, their specific requirements, and their potential value to the school. He bemoaned the destruction of so many tulip poplars, the most valuable tree in Appalachia, and recommended that sassafras be cleared to allow the remaining poplars to grow; he mourned the sloppy way white oaks had been cut, and he was disgusted by the worm decay in the old chestnut trees.

"I knew by heart every acre of land, and, literally, knew the trees individually, and what I thought ought to be done with them," he wrote in his letter of resignation in 1909.[3] In that letter he urged the school to keep buying land, predicting that with sustainable management the forests would appreciate in both value and usefulness. Mason was right on the mark.

In addition to educational opportunities and labor assignments for students, and recreation for all, the Berea Forest has enjoyed a revenue stream far beyond anything Mason could have ever imagined.[4] Berea was the first college in America to sell the carbon credits from its forest in a landmark cap-and-trade deal.

SELLING TREES TO SAVE THEM

Cap-and-trade systems aim to reduce greenhouse gas emissions. Not all environmentalists believe they are the best way to address the challenge, but for the time being they are the best option around. Designed to incentivize companies to use nonpolluting sources of energy by increasing the cost of *not* doing so, states or nations that have such a system set an annual limit on carbon emissions for some industries. That allowance is the cap. If industries with caps, such as utility companies, need to emit more carbon dioxide, they can "buy" credits from a company or an organization that does not use or want its carbon to "off-set" the difference. That's the trade.

Forests can serve as a trade in a cap-and-trade system because trees store carbon dioxide. The more they store—and there's disagreement on how long a mature tree will store carbon dioxide—the healthier the environment. When the state of California established the first cap-and-trade system in America in 2013, Berea entered the market.

"There's green in being green, and that's true of colleges, too," said Vice President Singleton.

In such a system, the price of carbon is set by the market, but the estimation of the value of forests is time-consuming, highly technical, and expensive work; Berea worked with New Forests, an Australian company, that agreed to underwrite those expenses as well as find potential buyers.

"New Forests got the ethos of Berea," said Singleton.

In 2019, after several years of intensive fieldwork, Berea received a check for $3.3 million, an initial payment for the old-growth trees that the college had never cut down and a down payment on many of the younger trees the college will not cut down for at least ninety-nine years. In addition to that first large payment, the college might realize as much as $250,000 annually for the foreseeable future, and it can continue to harvest some of the trees. All the revenues will support the educational and recreational activities at the forest.

"The carbon project," said Clint Patterson, the Berea forester, "can be viewed as a reward for Berea's long history of responsible forest management."

BEREA'S GREEN PROMISES KEPT

Back in 2007, some 336 college and university leaders signed a pledge to reduce their institutions' carbon footprints. Berea signed and then outlined *how* it would reduce consumption of natural resources and decrease its use of nonrenewable fossil fuels. It committed itself to creating a culture of sustainability on campus and sharing good practices with the wider community. In just ten years, Berea received a gold star in the environmental scorecard of higher education institutions throughout the United States.

Berea has nine LEED-certified buildings, five with certifiably sustainable wood, including the Margaret Cargill Natural Sciences and Health Building and Shinn Hall, one of several environmentally sound residential halls.[5] Home to 124 students, the three-story Shinn Hall is clad in recycled brick and heated and cooled with geothermal wells. Windows, lighting, paint, flooring, and water systems all meet the highest environmental standards, and all the windows and doorframes came from Berea timber not included in the cap-and-trade program. It was cut and milled by staff and students. Aaron Beale, director of Student Craft, adds, "Students and staff made the oak desks, dressers, and occasional tables for Shinn Hall, and [it] is a point of great pride on campus and within the program." Brandon Noble ('16) was one of those students. His first labor assignment at Berea was woodworking.

"I'm a kid from Harlem and knew nothing about wood. I'm no artist, but I loved it and, boy, did I learn to appreciate the creativity that goes into making something so nice and so functional," he said on the phone from his home in Mesa, Arizona. "It's no testament to me, but a huge one to the leadership at Berea."[6]

In addition to the forest, the farm, and green buildings, Berea offers numerous transportation options for students, including a bike rental business and five bike repair stations around campus. It has a pool of cars for students, like nurses or community service volunteers, who need to get to work sites; it has a car sharing program—a fee with one person, free with two or more—and it runs a van to the local shopping mall.

The college pushes zero-waste events. I attended one lunch sponsored by the Office of Sustainability on campus. About one hundred representatives from all departments and centers were present. After we served ourselves, staff and labor students presented data about food waste and how to reduce it at large gatherings; the comparative costs and advantages to various recyclable utensils and plates; and information on composting and recycling with offers to help organize all such events.

SUSTAINABILITY IN THE CLASSROOM

Changing the culture also demands educating students. "If you are not educating students about sustainability, why bother?" said Joan Pauly, former director of Berea's Office of Sustainability.

At Berea, Rachel Hidding ('21), sunny and open, was elected student president of the Office of Sustainability. An agriculture and natural resources major, she had studied permafrost in Alaska, ecofarming in Hawaii, and soil science in Malaysia, and her final labor position was managing the Green Office Certification Program. In that role, she helped academic departments and dormitories source green products, make sensible purchases, conserve water and energy, recycle and reuse, and compete campus-wide for the green ribbon.

After her graduation in 2021, Rachel landed a summer internship back in Alaska, working on a lion's mane mushroom farm and living in a 1985 Toyota Dolphin camper "with all the original furnishings," she happily reports.

Although student engagement on sustainability at Berea extends into extracurriculars and labor assignments, it starts in the classroom.

"Students often come thinking sustainability means recycling, maybe solar panels," said Compton Professor of Sustainability Nancy Gift. "But at Berea we approach sustainability as a lens, not a discipline. We try to find the good in all things, even weeds."

A Harvard- and Cornell-trained biologist and soil scientist, Gift teaches introduction to sustainability, introduction to agriculture, and the history of women and Black farmers in Kentucky. She works with professors to develop relevant courses in sustainability—everything from the ecology of weeds to *Pavement: Fractured*, a public art piece done in the cracks of a parking lot by studio art students. By 2020, 53 percent of all Berea graduates were exposed to at least one course in sustainability in half of all thirty-two academic departments, and the numbers keep growing.

But, as Gift said about environmental education, "telling people they are going to Hell doesn't change their minds," and she cited Berea's Ecovillage. "People don't live at Ecovillage because they are green, but by living there they might become green."

Designed by the legendary environmental architect Sim Van der Ryn, the complex, which opened in 2004, has fifty two-story environmentally sound apartments for nontraditional students, primarily single mothers with one or two children. With individual garden plots, an on-site water purification system, and a shared permaculture "food forest," the residents satisfy their labor requirements by composting, gardening, babysitting for one another, and governing themselves. And thinking holistically, the college opened its Boyd and Gaynell Fowler Child Development Lab, where education and child and family studies majors do their supervised "student teaching" or conduct research with preschoolers from Ecovillage in Ecovillage.

GREEN HYDROPOWER AND INNOVATIVE PARTNERS

About thirty-five miles east of Ecovillage, not far from the town of Ravenna, the college has broken other new ground, heading toward another promise kept. It built and owns two hydroelectric power plants.

For a long time, coal extracted in eastern Kentucky traveled north by barge along the narrow and meandering Kentucky River. Eventually railroads and later highways rendered all river commerce obsolete, and by 2002 most of the locks and dams on the polluted and unused Kentucky River were abandoned. In 2012, the US Department of Energy released a report that said many dams, particularly small ones, could produce hydroelectric power, if repurposed. But nothing happened anywhere until David Kinloch, a mechanical engineer, a committed environmentalist, and president of Appalachian Hydro Associates (AHA), saw the potential for doing just that along the Kentucky River. He needed a financial partner who shared his vision of a clean environment and a commitment to the area, so he approached Berea.

Choosing to work with creative partners who share its values seems to be one tangible way Berea maintains its commitment to both its principles and innovation. AHA was such a partner. Berea financed the $10 million project, combining its own money with available tax credits, and in October 2021 it became the first institution of higher education in the United States to open a hydroelectric power plant. They named it the Matilda Hamilton Fee Hydroelectric Station in honor of the fearless wife of John G. Fee.

With several six-foot-tall mainframe computers, housed in a concrete bunker high above the riverbank, the plant uses variable speed technology, a first in hydroelectric power generation. The computers control five underwater turbines that operate when water is high enough, and slow down or stop completely when the water is too low. No greenhouse gasses are ever emitted.

"It demonstrates that local green initiatives can be financially feasible, create reliable sources of income at an acceptable rate of return, and shows our students—and everyone else—the viability of state-of-the-art renewable energy technologies," said President Roelofs.

Lock 12 lies in rural Estill County, where the poverty rate is 31 percent, so the college sells the electricity it generates to a not-for-profit member cooperative established in 1938 under the New Deal.

"This power represents a significant savings for 1,500 households plus all our 52,000 members who will see a 6 percent reduction in their overall energy bills," said Carol Wright, CEO of the Jackson Energy Cooperative.

Furthermore, the Matilda Fee power plant offsets 50 percent of the college's electrical use, and in 2024, when Berea and AHA cut the ribbon on a second hydroelectric power plant at Lock 14, the college will offset 100 percent of its electrical use and sell the remaining inexpensive power to low-income people in Kentucky.

Meanwhile, as the turbines and their generators spin out electricity, the Berea computer engineering students and their professors dream about robots. The state requires all organic material, such as twigs and logs, to stay in the river, but the other stuff—milk bottles, deflated basketballs, and worn tires—can muck up the works. What if a robot with a long arm and a prehensile hand, driven by artificial intelligence, could differentiate a bottle from a branch, pick it up, and throw it into a dumpster on shore?

"No progress yet," President Roelofs said, laughing, "but it's another way to connect academics with our Great Commitments."

10

SERVING APPALACHIA AND ITS PEOPLE

To engage Appalachian communities, families, and students in
partnership for mutual learning, growth, and service.

Most colleges and universities understand that they need to be—
and should be—responsible neighbors. International conferences and national matrixes encourage and facilitate best practices, and examples are numerous: a university expands into a poor adjacent neighborhood and negotiates a multimillion-dollar fund for the area as recompense for displacement. Colleges invest endowment funds with an eye toward diversity, equity, and sustainability. Many colleges purchase goods and services locally whenever possible. Others open their facilities to neighbors, invite communities to programs, and support lifelong learning, and some incubate local businesses. Some engage in more ambitious economic and educational development projects: one, the Wisconsin Idea, is a statewide extension program on steroids.

Berea has been at community engagement since 1873. Its first president, E. Henry Fairchild, distributed books, established Sunday schools in neighboring areas, and, in his final address, outlined the needs of communities that in many ways still influence Berea's Eighth Great Commitment. The school's long and multifaceted presence resides in both its immediate neighborhood and throughout central Appalachia. Those initiatives have included Fireside Industries, the Council of the Southern Mountains, Pine Mountain Settlement School, Opportunity Schools, Partners for Education,

Grow Appalachia, Brushy Fork Institute, and the Appalachian Fund. The list goes on and on.

EVOLUTION OF SOME COMMUNITY INITIATIVES

Like Berea itself, the commitment is historic, and its various expressions have evolved over time. The early Fireside Industries, for instance, changed as the market changed and Berea's own internal Student Craft program grew. The Conference of Southern Mountain Workers, started in 1913, laid the groundwork for much of the War on Poverty, and morphed and merged with another organization before finally closing its doors.

Sometimes new programs replicated older ones. In 1986, Jane Stephenson, wife of President John Stephenson, resuscitated Berea's unique Opportunity Schools (1925–1946), modeled after Danish folk schools that were free three-week campus-based learning experiences for twenty-five to forty adults—often parents or grandparents of Berea students—of "inquiring minds and cooperative spirits" who, on average, had eighth- or ninth-grade educations. Hundreds of people participated over two decades.

In the new iteration, the New Opportunity School for Women, women came to Berea, free of charge, and attended special classes on health, geography, music, leadership, and career development, with the weekend devoted to building self-esteem. Stella Parton, Dolly's younger sister and a successful singer and actress in her own right, was a weekend volunteer for many years. She offered inexpensive beauty tips, such as using mayonnaise to shine hair, Crisco to soften skin, and Vaseline to brighten eyes, and then she'd take everyone to Goodwill to buy new outfits, complimenting their best colors. On Sundays, she described on the phone to me from her home in Nashville, "we'd have a fashion show . . . pouring love and positive energy into each other." In 1996, Berea spun off the New Opportunity School for Women, which became its own freestanding not-for-profit organization that is still existent, promoting lifelong learning.

The most recent Berea spin-off is the groundbreaking Partners for Education (PFE). With bits of its current mission rooted in earlier projects as well as the Harlem Children's Zone, but adapted for rural communities, PFE, led by Dreama Gentry ('89), focused on cradle-to-career community development in the thirty poorest counties of central Appalachia, the counties decimated by the slow death of the coal industry. PFE raised and distributed millions of dollars from the state and federal government every year; in 2021, it raised $42 million to support early childhood and literacy programs, professional development for teachers and rural librarians, and arts education. Having become a model for all rural America, not just Appalachia, the college spun it off in July 2022 and renamed it Partners for Rural Impact (PRI). Teri Thompson, Berea's Vice President for Strategic Initiatives, helped guide the transition.

COAL EMPLOYMENT PROJECT

Couple this ongoing commitment to central Appalachia with Berea's ethos of service and it is easy to find "ordinary students doing extraordinary things back in their communities." Betty Jean Hall ('68) was one such student. Born in the hollows outside the small town of Buckhorn in Perry County in eastern Kentucky, Hall moved to Berea as a young girl when her father, a woodworker, was hired to teach in the college's industrial arts department.[1] Her classmate, Sharyn Mitchell, former librarian in Berea's Special Collections and Archives, remembered her as "a pistol, who never accepted no for an answer."

After Hall graduated from the college with a degree in history, she moved north, saying on the phone with a chuckle, "I was not physically coordinated, but I could type like a whiz." She worked at a Washington, DC, law firm and then went to the Appalachian Regional Commission (ARC), one of the few Appalachians hired—most of them from Berea College. After three years at ARC, when Hall infuriated her boss and went outside the agency to find $160 to buy schoolbooks for four impoverished fatherless children in Pike County, Kentucky, her job was "phased out."

"The kids got the books and I got gone," she laughs. She enrolled in law school. In 1977, a woman in Tennessee was denied a tour of a coal mine with her male colleagues, and outraged, she called her friend Betty Jean Hall. With 99.8 percent of all miners being men and 97.8 percent of all administrative jobs in mining companies being held by men, she said to Hall, "we must do something."

Coal mining was one of the best-paying jobs in Appalachia, even though many mining families struggled financially, a situation made worse by the fact that the only jobs available to women were in fast-food restaurants or babysitting. No laws prohibited women from working in mines, but as mines went deeper and deeper, sometimes with labyrinthine passages stretching two or more miles, disasters were all too common—roof collapses, explosions, and fires. Those conditions only exacerbated a hypermasculine culture that believed women in mines were both unfit and bad luck. "That was a lot of bunk, but that superstition sure made a nice excuse for the operators," Hall said pointedly.

In 1968 President Lyndon Johnson had signed an executive order that prohibited job discrimination based on gender by any company that received $50,000 or more of federal money and ordered the development of affirmative action plans; however, companies ignored the order, and no federal agency policed it. So, just one year out of law school, Hall began the not-for-profit Coal Employment Project (CEP) to force its implementation.

With one employee, one volunteer, and a small grant from the nascent Ms. Foundation for Women, Hall traveled throughout

Appalachia. She spoke to the few women who had found jobs with mining companies and many others, including many single mothers. They talked about their lives, their families, their dreams, and their needs. She heard repeatedly that they would—and could—do mining work, if given training and a chance.

In May 1978, Betty Jean Hall, a wisp of a woman with a radiant smile and "hair as dark as bituminous coal," as one reporter wrote, filed formal complaints against 153 mining companies in Kentucky, Tennessee, Virginia, and West Virginia. Together the companies produced 50 percent of all the coal produced in America, and they all had federal contracts.

Within days of the filing, the US Department of Labor announced it would review the complaints, and soon Consolidation Coal, the second-largest coal company in the entire United States, capitulated. It paid $370,000 in back pay to seventy-eight women and, even more significantly, agreed to hire one woman for every four men until it reached 20 percent of its workforce. Hall's CEP had won a major victory.

CEP negotiated many settlements, and within a year some 2,600 women were working in mines, many going from making $2.50 an hour babysitting to $7.90 an hour working in the mines. By 1981, when Hall won the prestigious Rockefeller Public Service Award (about a month after giving birth to twins), 12 percent of all entry-level positions underground had gone to women.

"I don't know if I was making history, but I know I was making a living," Marilyn Vanderfleet, a coal miner from Harlan, Kentucky, said to a documentary filmmaker.[2]

Hall stayed at CEP for ten years, monitoring progress on the legal front, ensuring proper training for the women miners, organizing annual national conferences, and building a strong relationship with the United Mine Workers. They worked together on mine safety and sexual harassment, including a notorious case of men peeping at women in their restrooms.[3] Then, in an exquisite twist, Hall was appointed chair and chief judge of the Department of Labor's Benefits Review Board, responsible for hearing appeals on worker compensation claims, including those for black lung benefits for miners.

"It was something that needed to be done," Hall, now retired, said about CEP from her home in Cary, North Carolina. "And in many ways, those wonderful people I met at Berea are the reason I got into coal mining."

COAL MINING TO TOURISM

But just as women began to break into coal mining, the business began to change. With new technologies, coal companies increased production by blasting off mountaintops to expose seams of coal. Gargantuan machines with massive shovels lumber across the naked mountaintop from open seam to open seam and gobble up one hundred tons of coal in each obscene mouthful. They dump the leftover rock and dirt into valleys and streams below and dispose of the coal waste—sometimes called gob or tailings—in man-made "ponds" the coal companies dig and then often abandon. It's cheaper to pay for desertion than to clean up the gob.

"They call West Virginia 'almost Heaven,' and it is, until the coal industry bombs your home," said Judy Bonds in Whitesville, West Virginia.

An estimated five hundred mountains in Appalachia have been desecrated.[4] And with them has also come the decimation of the coal mining jobs. In 1979, about 55,000 coal miners worked in Kentucky, and by 2016 that the number was down to 6,612.[5] Far fewer people are needed to find and extract the coal.

The slow death of coal mining initially spurred impractical economic development efforts. National companies received tax incentives to open factories just as globalization fueled competition and moved jobs overseas; the companies that did open hired fewer workers at low wages, resulting in lower tax bases and causing further environmental and societal degradation. The quixotic vision of industrial pockets did not play to the strengths of central Appalachia—its people, its land, and its beauty—but tourism might.[6] Tourism development has begun in eastern Kentucky.

Working with disparate communities to stimulate recreational biking fits neatly into Berea's Eighth Commitment of engaging with allies for the betterment of the region as well as liberal education and sustainability. For several years Berea's Entrepreneurship for the Public Good (EPG) has focused student participants on tourism. In particular, on long-distance biking and how it could enrich the mix of travel options in the mountains and forests of Kentucky.

Hired in 2007 to design and implement an entrepreneurial leadership program for nonbusiness majors, Peter Hackbert, a triathlete, dreamt of extending bike trails all the way to the Ohio River and connecting them to the Underground Railroad Bicycle Route.[7] He retired in the summer of 2022, but his work on bike trails continues. EPG selects twenty students each year to participate in teams over two consecutive summers to understand the economic and cultural dynamics of tourism development and then work with local communities to advance their goals. Katie Roach ('22) was selected for one cohort.

"I applied to EPG because everyone seemed to have fun. They worked together, seemed tightly knit, and were comfortable with public speaking, which I wasn't," said the personable studio art major with a minor in sustainability from Oak Ridge, Tennessee.

As members of EPG, she and her colleagues earned two course credits and a labor salary, attended conferences, made public presentations, visited the officially designated Trail Towns in Appalachia, and interviewed long-distance bikers, hikers, and rock climbers to understand their preferences, their pleasures, their needs, and their typical expenses.

"We learned that bikers hate the dogs, but they sure love the beauty of Kentucky," she said, laughing.

Over several years, EPG cohort members amassed inventories of the counties' natural and man-made assets; they mapped historical sites and scenic lookouts, ATMs, bed-and-breakfasts, restaurants, and bike shops. They studied local attractions, special events, and their respective economic advantages in towns around Appalachia. They compared different social media platforms and offered workshops in their use to local businesses. They worked to understand destination management, promotion, and marketing, and the teams plotted the Daniel Boone Bike Route through five distressed counties and completed the necessary applications for national certification for three towns to join the growing network of economically viable Trail Towns.

One bike route (USBR 76) goes east to west through the town of Berea and joins four Trail Towns in eastern Kentucky. The other is an overlay of the original Daniel Boone Trace, carved in 1775 from the Cumberland Gap to Boonesborough, Kentucky. It became the second nationally certified bike route (USBR 21) connecting Atlanta to Cleveland.

"If it weren't for these kids, we wouldn't be where we are now," said John Fox, founder of Friends of Boone Trace, which works to preserve segments of that historic trail.

Over "the COVID summer," Katie Roach, stuck at home and unable to experience EPG's fieldwork, wrote and produced a promotional video of businesses along one section of the Boone Trace, using Google maps, social media reviews, and interviews with users. Although Roach hopes to become a landscape architect, in the meantime, she used her EPG training to help her widowed mother renovate and promote a small house on family land in Rockwood, Tennessee, as a bed-and-breakfast.

"I'll identify the potential market and promote it, and maybe it will become our primary source of income," said a confident Roach.

BEREA'S MOUNTAIN PARTNERS

Ever since President E. Henry Fairchild (1869–1889) started distributing books to surrounding communities, every Berea president has embraced—beyond the students the college serves—a commitment to central Appalachia. President Francis Hutchins once said, "We have never been a college limited to a campus; if it had been so limited it would not be the Berea we know."

"Ignoring the environment that sends students to Berea would only add to the challenge of ending cycles of poverty," offers Candace Mullins, executive director of Berea's Grow Appalachia, one of several Berea-funded projects that works with community organizations throughout the region. Scott Christian Care Center in Oneida, Tennessee, is one such partner.

About ninety miles south of Berea, just south of the Kentucky border, located down a commercial strip of fast-food restaurants and auto repair shops, Scott Christian Care Center (SCCC) occupies an old warehouse, next to the Goodwill and a Dollar General store. I spotted the large cross on the side of the two-story building, just as Lisa Cotton, its founder and executive director, told me I would.

An effervescent middle-aged force, Cotton grew up in Oneida, a town of about 3,500 people scattered over ten square miles. Her parents both worked in the Dollar General store—her mother still does. Cotton went off to college and trained as an industrial engineer, returned to Oneida, married, worked, and began to volunteer in a battered women's shelter.

"I saw the impact of women having absolutely no essentials. No toilet paper, no diapers, no soap, no toothpaste. I hesitated to tell my pastor, fearful he would not believe the needs were so great, but the poverty haunted me. I started a small not-for-profit on the side to collect and distribute donations," she said as we sat in her nondescript office just behind a small lending library.

To learn how to run a not-for-profit organization, she turned to Berea's Brushy Fork Institute. Begun in 1988 by President John Stephenson, Brushy Fork "strengthens local and grassroots leaders by building on their interests and giving them new skills to work effectively in groups," said Donna Daniels, the executive director and a 1989 Berea graduate from Kingsport, Tennessee.

On my way to Oneida, I visited Greg Lakes, a retired manager from Lowes, the home improvement chain, who had also participated in a Brushy Fork workshop soon after he retired and with his wife turned a modern, comfortable home outside the town of Berea into the Clover Bottom Bed and Breakfast.

"We worked in small groups," Lakes said about the workshop. "We talked about what problems we saw in our county and what might help small businesses the most. We all agreed the big problem is trash. In these parts there's no garbage pickup. If you can afford it, you hire a private service, but most can't afford it and dump their trash any old place, including the streams."

The group, many of whom Lakes was meeting for the first time, decided they first had to raise awareness of the issue and thought it'd be good to get the local fishermen involved. He explained, "Fishermen will make strong advocates in the community. We're recruiting local fishermen to parade down the main street of our county seat, carrying full garbage bags right to the transfer station."

The group then devised catchy taglines: "Company's coming, let's prepare" and "Take pride in where you reside."

"People in these parts take hospitality serious," Lakes said. "I'm going to dress up as a fish," he added with a smile.

With just a germ of an idea, Lisa Cotton from Oneida took workshops in grant writing, branding, volunteer recruitment, budgeting, and finance at the Brushy Fork Institute at Berea. Eventually, feeling more confident, in 2009 she left her job and now, with just one full-time employee, runs SCCC. With volunteers from throughout the area, SCCC offers a free medical clinic for the uninsured, run by a doctor from Knoxville; a food pantry that serves about five thousand people, 30 percent of whom are children; a free dental clinic; and a personal hygiene pantry. SCCC offers a range of regularly scheduled support groups, including Alcoholics Anonymous and a widows group, as well as parenting, financial planning, and nutrition classes. As befits a town that has fourteen churches in it, SCCC provides those services "dedicated to the Lord for His Work, for His People, and for His Glory."

Cotton also convinced the Recovery/Drug Court to locate in the SCCC building, and its rent now supports the entire mortgage. In 2022, SCCC opened a bright, fully equipped, long-term residence on the second floor of the space where eight women, referred by the Recovery Court, stay for eight to ten months. The women—along with two trustees from the local jail—help the center every day in a variety of appropriate ways, including the construction of a theater that is used by the town for community events and that is partially supported by the Berea College Appalachian Fund. It abuts the commercial kitchen that SCCC manages for people eager to prepare foods for sale at farmers' markets. Many of them are members of Berea's Grow Appalachia, which supplied the funds to build the commercial kitchen.

GROW APPALACHIA

With the enthusiasm and financial support from entrepreneur John Paul DeJoria, who learned about hunger in eastern Kentucky from a colleague, David Cooke ('82) began Grow Appalachia in 2009.

"It struck me that there were fewer and fewer gardens even though malnutrition, food security, and hunger issues are more striking every year," Cooke said.

For thirteen years, he had worked as an extension agent with small landowners back in his home state of West Virginia before returning to Berea. Grow Appalachia has a simple mission with a large mandate: help low-income Appalachians achieve food security and better health through good nutrition

Now led by Cooke's protégée, Candace Mullins, Grow Appalachia has helped almost 20,000 gardeners grow more than 5.5 million pounds of organic vegetables. During COVID-19, Grow Appalachia also fed more than 400,000 kids when schools were shut down. With tentacles throughout all of central Appalachia, the program funds workshops, commercial kitchens, farmers' markets, and garden coordinators. SCCC benefits from this partnership, as do thirty other community groups, including Red Bird Mission in Beverly, Kentucky.

Driving alongside an old, rusted rail line that snakes in and out of the woods, I kept spotting derelict coal mines with corroded tipples peeking through the thick forests. I was heading about ninety-five miles northeast of Oneida and some one hundred miles from Berea to Beverly, Kentucky, home of Red Bird Mission. Established in 1921 by evangelical missionaries, Red Bird Mission appears unexpectedly like a small town off the narrow, winding road in this remote and impoverished area.

RED BIRD MISSION

A complex of one-story buildings in a widening of the hollow, Red Bird Mission provides medical and dental care and home improvements for people living high up in the hollows of three remote counties. Some 35 percent of the adults never graduated from high school, poverty ranges from 25 to 45 percent, no public sewer system exists, and telephone and electricity are unreliable. Red Bird Mission is the only safety net.

The mission runs a pre-K–12 school that includes twenty boarding students from Africa and Latin America. It offers life skill classes, a large thrift shop, and a farmers' market. It runs work camps all year, where volunteers arrive and work to repair

Aerial view of Red Bird Mission, Beverly, Kentucky. Courtesy of Red Bird Mission.

trailers and houses in the hollows. New mothers take monthly parenting classes, with a bag of baby necessities given out after each class, and volunteers stock well-organized shelves of toys, books, new clothes, and new shoes that will stuff Christmas boxes for the children of their ten thousand clients. In 2023 it added telehealth services by installing Starlink in thirty homes in the Red Bird Mission region, including homes of the elderly, the disabled, and low-income families.

"Red Bird Mission does a deep dive into lives . . . we want to build relationships and acknowledge the value and the worth in all our clients that will lead to confidence and self-sufficiency," said Tracy Nolan, director of community outreach. A nurse by training, she arrived at Red Bird Mission from Louisville in 1996, having won a yearlong community health fellowship. She never left.

One of her many responsibilities is to help recruit participants for Grow Appalachia. Many Red Bird Mission clients drive forty-five minutes or more to the closest grocery store, but many have long since lost the know-how to grow their own food. They lack resources, confidence, and support. Every participant in all Grow Appalachia projects must attend six workshops on mountain gardening, taught by a local coordinator. The workshops include everything from soil health to pest control to high tunnels. At the end, each gardener receives organic fertilizer, tools, seeds, and plants to start a garden, and the coordinator provides assistance tilling and individualized follow-up help as needed.

Red Bird Mission joined Grow Appalachia in 2010 and each year strives to recruit fifty-five members, of whom twenty-five are new family gardeners. Anyone who wants to return for a second year can do so if they agree to participate in the farmers' market that Red Bird Mission manages. Their data show that Grow Appalachia gardeners use the Red Bird Mission food pantry less than before they joined.

Daugh and Joyce Sizemore, an elderly couple, live in the hills way above Red Bird Mission somewhere in Clay County. Raising bees was a family tradition, but since joining Grow Appalachia they also now make honey and sell it, grow walnuts and sell them, and grow sorghum and make syrup. Joyce bakes and sells pastries, too.

Sometimes the Sizemores work in the commercial kitchen at Red Bird Mission—also supported by Berea's Grow Appalachia. The "salsa guy" often uses the kitchen, too. He took the workshop, started growing tomatoes and various peppers, and then signed up for a second year, wanting to try his hand at making salsa. Red Bird Mission then helped him get the required microprocessing certification, and Grow Appalachia provided a salsa starter kit with new jars, lids, and labels for his new business. In 2022, using the commercial kitchen, he, along with six other family gardeners, collectively made $9,154 at Red Bird Mission's year-round farmers' market—this in a county where 40 percent of the population live under the poverty line.

PINE MOUNTAIN SETTLEMENT SCHOOL

Preston Jones, a lanky and bearded plant and soil scientist whose mother and grandmother both attended Berea, was the director of the Pine Mountain Settlement School (PMSS), about forty winding miles away from Red Bird Mission in Harlan County. Each year, Jones and the staff of environmental educators and craftspeople welcome about three thousand people, including more than two thousand schoolchildren, to the bucolic campus of one thousand acres. The school groups spend several days on site, hiking the trails, prowling for owls at night, looking for critters in the streams, spinning and weaving wool, and square dancing after dinner in one of the twenty-five lovely sandstone and wooden buildings that dot the center.

"They come from as far away as Alabama," said Jones. "We had one kid who had never touched a tree. Imagine what an experience this was for him."

Begun in 1913, PMSS traces its inspiration back to Toynbee Hall in London and Hull House in Chicago, the urban settlement houses established to educate new immigrants. With support from the Kentucky Federation of Women's Clubs, Katherine Pettit and May Stone founded Hindman Settlement School and stayed there for many years. Eventually, a local man in Bledsoe, Kentucky, lured Pettit away to open a self-sustaining boarding school for isolated mountain children at Pine Mountain. The school remained active until 1949, when a public school rendered it redundant.

Then PMSS turned to Berea College to help it envision a useful future for the land and its facilities. PMSS redefined itself as a community-based, multifaceted center for environmental and cultural education. Four members of the seventeen-member board are always affiliated with Berea College, including whoever is president of the college at the time. The college gives no direct support to PMSS, but PMSS regularly participates in Grow Appalachia for its neighbors, the Brushy Fork Institute for its staff, and often receives grants from Berea's Appalachian Fund for special projects.

THE APPALACHIAN FUND

Unlike the kid from Alabama who spent time at PMSS, Tyler Boggs ('23) grew up in Whitesburg, Kentucky, and knows the mountains and its trees well. When we met over lunch at the local Mexican restaurant in Whitesburg, it was the summer of his junior year. He was back home, running the Cowan Community Action Group's summer camp program.

Responsible for 320 kids, Boggs designed the program (divided among eight weeklong sessions), handled all administrative details, and supervised nine student staff members. A major in elementary education, Boggs was intent on returning to Whitesburg, where qualified, certified teachers, particularly men, are desperately needed. Because he was spending the summer in his hometown, working for a not-for-profit organization relevant to his major, Berea's Office of Internships and Career Development supported his paid placement, and Berea's Appalachian Fund gave the funds to pay all the camp counselors.

The Appalachian Fund was founded by Herbert Faber, an unassuming engineer, who, along with a colleague, invented Formica. In the 1950s, when the post–World War II housing boom took off, the colorful, durable, and ubiquitous material on kitchen counters made Faber a fortune. The factory was in Cincinnati.

Faber, or so the story goes, had noticed a pattern—individual employees, if they ever asked to take an unpaid day off, which was rare, would request Monday or Friday, and Faber wondered why.

Leaving their families behind, most of Faber's employees came from the mountains of central Appalachia. Medical services were rare in that part of the country, so if a relative got sick, the employee would need to leave work, drive or, more likely, take a bus to somewhere close to home, wend his way to the hollow, borrow a car or truck, pick up the sick person, drive maybe hours on poor roads that wound through the mountains to the nearest clinic, then wait, drive the relative home, and make it back to Cincinnati in time for his next shift.

Hearing this, Faber and his wife established the Appalachian Fund in 1950 to support nursing programs, including Berea's, and medical clinics throughout the region. When the foundation ceased operations in 1987, their son gave the foundation's remaining assets to Berea College, asking that the funds continue to support health and education in the mountains. Five million dollars has grown to $14 million. Every year one part-time staff person—now Davey King—distributes about $500,000 from the Appalachian Fund to grassroots organizations in eastern Kentucky, Tennessee, and West Virginia for projects initiated and managed by local organizations.

Maybe those motorcyclists gave a collective thumbs' up to the tour group at the motel in the Cumberland Gap because of Berea's Appalachian Fund, the college's admissions' policy, the free tuition, the Labor Program, Grow Appalachia, the Brushy Fork Institute, the Bonner Scholars, or Partners for Rural Impact—or maybe because of all of it.

"People in Appalachia know Berea has been here, caring for a long time," said Teri Thompson, Berea's Vice President for Strategic Initiatives. Or, as Tyler Boggs, the future teacher in Whitesburg, said, "Berea is everywhere and helps connect me back to the mountains that I love so much."

CONCLUSION

When I first met Lyle Roelofs in the early days of his presidency, I asked him what he hoped to do during his tenure at Berea. "Keep Berea, Berea," he answered simply. When he announced his retirement more than eleven years later, someone on the Zoom call asked if he thought there would be changes at Berea. He responded, "No one can say that there won't be, but as an earlier Berea president once said, 'Berea changes presidents more than presidents change Berea.'"

In the spring of 2023, when the Berea Board introduced Dr. Cheryl Nixon, the tenth president of Berea and its first woman head, to the college community, she cited the significance of the Eight Great Commitments. Like her, I believe they are the strength of the college. Its radical roots are deep, its traditions strong, and its goals clear. John Fee knew exactly what he was doing, and everyone I met on campus, even those who couldn't rattle off the eight, honors his heroic commitment to equity and his strong support for a broad education for all.

Today, just as before, Berea bucks the trend: it stays small as other institutions grow. It holds the liberal arts dear as professional majors multiply. It has attained remarkable racial, gender, ethnic, and religious diversity as most institutions have just begun. It has built an enviable endowment, but unlike its financial peers, spends the interest only on its students. It prioritizes teaching and advising over research, and it maintains its regional focus even as it embraces the global. It supports communities that send most of its students and it unabashedly talks about love and respect. Unlike any other college anywhere in the country, and perhaps in the world, it educates only low-income students, and it offers every one of them free tuition—and has done so since 1892.

Twenty-eight years after beginning that no-tuition promise, Berea's Board recognized that to continue that commitment, it needed a large endowment. The college aggressively began to build one and has never stopped. Impressed by the college's values and its results, thousands of donors from the famous to the modest have given, and in return the college has managed those funds wisely. Today, Berea has an impressive endowment for any school, but particularly a small one that only educates low-income students.

The interest from those funds pays for 75 percent of the cost of educating each student, and the college raises the difference every year. Although it would make its fundraising challenge easier, the college does not accept tuition-paying students, seek the children of rich donors, or accept legacies or give athletic scholarships. But Berea is hardly the "richest" college. Some ninety-five colleges and universities have larger endowments, and yet, proportionally, they all enroll far smaller percentages of low-income students. Most richly endowed colleges don't have the will, and the others don't have the resources.

Most colleges rely on tuition as their primary revenue source. It is their business model. The dramatic rise in costs began in the 1980s, and consequently, tuition skyrocketed. In 2022, the average debt incurred by a graduate of a four-year private institution was about $30,000. Most troubling, Berea writes, women owe two-thirds of outstanding student debt; first-generation college students are twice as likely to be behind in their loan payments; and Black students on average still owe 95 percent of their student debt some twenty years out, compared to 6 percent of their white counterparts. Berea students, by all measures, are in those cohorts. But in 2022, 62 percent of all Berea graduates—all of them Pell eligible—graduated with zero debt; the other half graduated with less than $2,000. Think about that.

And what is the value of free? Statistically, only 11 percent of low-income, first-generation college students graduate from college, yet two-thirds of the recent Berea graduating classes are first-generation students. When asked what is the value of free, some alumni said it meant pursuing a career that they loved, no matter the salary. Others went on for advanced degrees, and still more entered—and stayed—in public or community service; one said, point-blank, he was able to buy a house. The value of free not only strengthens individuals but helps society, too.

Berea's endowment and its private donors, and federal and state grants, particularly the Pell grants, make low debt loads possible, but so, too, does Berea's Labor Program. The integration of labor and learning has been a Berea goal since its earliest days. John Fee and his colleagues understood that slavery had dehumanized the enslaved and degraded manual labor. The dignity of labor—all labor—became a fundamental goal of Berea. Its by-product might be a lessening of student debt, but its fundamental purpose is to honor all jobs well done.

In the labor program, Berea students start by developing soft skills, such as teamwork, accountability, and initiative, and then in future assignments they learn managerial and other specialized skills in areas of their interests with trained supervisors guiding them. This is not ordinary work-study. There are nine federally approved work colleges, but Berea has achieved a level of academic excellence the others have not, and Berea is the only one with free tuition and an emphasis on students from low-income families. It's not an easy task, integrating labor and learning. Berea continually refines and improves its approach and tries hard to link students' academic interests with relevant skills, even with constantly changing professional landscapes. In 2019, an impressive 92 percent of Berea students said labor helped them develop academically, too.

Berea, of course, faces the challenges that other institutions of higher education confront: recruitment, retention, and mental health issues. Whether it's reverberations from the pandemic, divisive public dialogue, or anxiety about the future, Berea students are showing a greater need for mental health services. The college's efforts to deepen that support require additional fundraising as well as robust and coordinated internal communications. Although Berea does relatively well, compared to its peers, with retaining low-income students, it, too, faces the challenge of recruiting men. These obstacles cannot be addressed just with money; they are systemic and belie easy answers. Consequently, Berea assesses its own practices and participates in numerous associations that grapple with these national problems. Best practices will emerge from these collaborations and Berea, undoubtedly, will adopt and modify possible solutions for its own purposes.

So why is there only one Berea? I cannot answer that. Maybe others have tried and failed, and Berea would be the first to say that it has not achieved Fee's vision; there's still work to be done. Yes, you could take pieces of the model, but no institution can ever repeat Berea's dramatic history in that location. You certainly could—as some colleges now try to do—diversify student bodies, but as long as tuition remains the primary revenue source for most private colleges, true diversity of race, ethnicity, and class will be difficult to achieve.

Certainly other colleges exist that embrace equal opportunity and the importance of social mobility, but without financial resources, it is difficult for them to provide the services that low-income students often require or the experiences that would enrich their perspectives and help shape their dreams. Yes, you could shift tenure requirements and emphasize teaching and advising, as Berea does, but then the institutions might slip from the top of the research heap, another potential source of revenue and prestige. Yes, colleges might identify a new niche for themselves, and market that specialty to attract more students. Yes, colleges could raise funds for additional support services, but part of Berea's secret sauce lies in how those services are not add-ons, they are built into the college's DNA. Few Berea students appear ashamed of their poverty, academic deficits, or troubled and complicated families. To the contrary, the range of both direct and indirect supports for the students seems to encourage freethinking and confidence. Building community requires more than new buildings.

I once asked Lyle Roelofs: If he had a magic wand, where would he build a new Berea? He thought before answering, "Maybe in the Southwest for Latino kids. They don't have a college, specifically, for them," and then he added, "But of course the board would need to be made up of Catholics." He went straight to the need for foundational values.

So maybe it would be possible to start another Berea from scratch, and that takes us back to where we began. John Fee had no money, but he had a unique vision, based on his profoundly simple reading of basic Christian values. Love your neighbor as yourself, or what he called impartial love. It still drives the Berea community. It's not always easy, and it can be messy, as many at Berea have said to me; however, this small college in the hills of Kentucky certainly shows us the way to a kinder world, and for that, it is indeed a national treasure.

ACKNOWLEDGMENTS

I owe scores of people deep gratitude for the help and support they gave me as I worked on this book over many years. It starts, of course, with Chad and Lisa Berry, who led the tour in 2011 that inspired me. Ever generous with their time, thoughts, and hospitality, they introduced me to oodles of people on campus and took me on hikes in the Berea Forest and road trips to the knobs. They opened their wonderful home in the rolling hills outside of town every time I visited. The college is lucky to have them, and I am lucky to call them friends.

It's impossible to acknowledge everyone at Berea who helped, but it is striking how many people were open and friendly: students seemed unfazed when a stranger asked endless questions; professors were invariably game to have me attend their classes; and administrators from President Lyle Roelofs to the finance staff and mail clerks were generous with their time and insights. I am particularly indebted to the Admissions Office and its talented staff under the leadership of Luke Hodson, Channell Barbour at Student Services, and Reverend Dr. LeSette Wright, all of whom were particularly helpful.

I dipped into the archives of the handsome quarterly *Berea Magazine* many, many times, and I thank its editorial staff and an ever-changing roster of student writers and photographers. Likewise, I drew on the comprehensive data compiled meticulously by the Office of Institutional Research and Assessment and congratulate its staff for the data's accessibility. I take all responsibility for any inaccurate interpretations of the information.

I think I met most, if not all, of the directors of the various centers and services, who provide students with endless opportunities and me with insights about the college and its values. I loved visiting the forest, the farm, and the Student Craft program and marvel at the work they all do. If you have not seen the Berea College Student Craft Catalog, I urge you to do so. No catalog anywhere for anything has been more beautifully designed and produced.

The talented people, most of them Berea graduates, who maintain Berea's extensive network in central Appalachia introduced me to many of their partners. I claim no expertise on the complexities of Appalachia, but my visits to eastern Kentucky and northern Tennessee, thanks to the Berea folks, certainly enriched my understanding of the region and Berea's deep connections to it.

One of the delights of Berea is seeing students working at their labor positions every time you turn around—greeting you at the hotel, watering plants, restocking shelves, turning compost, delivering food, and weaving blankets. Berea busy is an apt description of Berea students, who juggle classes, homework, labor, and service. On several occasions in the library (when she did not know I was eavesdropping) I witnessed Sharyn Mitchell working with students as their labor supervisor and saw how valuable that piece is to Berea's overall success.

I spent lots of time hanging out and just listening at the Berea Coffee and Tea Co. counter, the Mountaineer Dining Hall, the Boone Tavern café and restaurant, the Berea Farm Store, and the Appalachian Center. I loved hearing first-time visitors to town, gobsmacked by the lovely campus, the forest, the farm, and the diversity of the student body. "Oh, I had heard of Berea, but I had no idea . . ." was a common refrain.

Back home, I have many to thank, too, starting with Alexandra Shelley, my smart and helpful editor, and Melanie Locay, manager at the Center for Research in the Humanities at the New York Public Library, where I was a writer-in-residence, using the resources of that remarkable place with a "key" to one of the quiet writers' rooms. I thank Libby Penner, the interlibrary loan librarian, and Ryan Biracree, the digital services librarian at the Desmond-Fish Library in Garrison, New York. I thank Alex Wardle, Ned York, Jack Goldstein, and Jonathan Mintz for reading—and, in some cases, listening—to early drafts of chapters and offering suggestions or helping with a phrase, a word, or a metaphor. Eileen Sullivan keyed into how I might strengthen my approach by highlighting the challenges all colleges now face and how Berea addresses them. My Brooklyn buddies—Susan Herman, Leslie Newman, Jeremy Travis, and Joel Copperman—listened to my endless stories, and Susan and Leslie both read bits and pieces, giving valuable feedback. Chatting with Mary and Morris Rossabi at their kitchen table on the Upper Westside is always warm and friendly, as are my conversations about Berea with Franci Wiener and Karen Blessen. My biweekly Zoom friends, Cathy McDowell and Marianne Gabel, were equally patient with my obsession, as were my sisters, Christina Mead and Alison Dykstra. My friends here in the Hudson Valley—Linda Lange, Kyle Good, Millie Solomon, Vicky Streitfeld, and the members of my kaffeeklatsch at Paulette's—humored me when Berea was on my mind.

But, most of all, I thank the talented students, past and present, whom I had the pleasure of talking with and, in most cases, meeting. Invariably, as we talked, I quickly forgot their "Berea stories" as I marveled at their optimism, curiosity, and decency. They gave me constant hope in an otherwise troubled world, or, as William Hutchins said, "they are ordinary people doing extraordinary things." Berea College is certainly the closest I have ever been to "a beloved community."

NOTES

1. BEREA TODAY

1. Appalachia stretches from south-central New York to Tupelo, Mississippi. Almost 30 million people live in the widely misunderstood region.

2. The Office of Institutional Research and Assessment at Berea collects these and other data used throughout the book.

3. Harvey Mudd, Pomona, William and Mary, and Wesleyan ranked above Berea.

4. Furthermore, it is one of *only* thirteen private colleges in America that received a Aaa rating in 2022 from Moody's.

2. JOHN FEE, HIS COURAGE, AND HIS CLARITY

1. Fee arrived at Lane several years after the charismatic student Theodore Weld had left. Weld had held eighteen controversial debates on whether slavery should be abolished immediately or gradually. Those debates tore Lane apart. By the time Fee arrived, Beecher, a gradualist himself, had rebuilt its reputation.

2. The Fees had six children, four of whom died before either of their parents.

3. An example is from Leviticus 25:45: "Moreover of the children of the strangers that do sojourn among you, of them shall ye buy, and of their families that are with you, which they begat in your land: and they shall be your possession" (King James Version). Berea's archives have Fee's "cut" Bible.

4. Herman Clay, an enslaved person on the Clay family estate near Richmond, Kentucky, named his son Cassius, whose own son became Cassius Clay Jr and later Muhammad Ali.

5. Some 180,000 Black men served in the Union army.

6. Fee was a prodigious writer, and from 1846 to 1881 the *American Missionary* magazine alone published 126 articles and letters by Fee, raising Berea's profile greatly.

7. Eventually, they moved back to Lexington and became pillars of the Black community there.

8. The law also stipulated that Blacks and whites could not study within twenty-five miles of one another.

9. *Berea's First 125 Years 1855–1980* by Elizabeth Peck and Emily Ann Smith describes those days vividly.

10. The reversal of the Day Law said that Black students could enroll at Berea if it offered majors not available at Kentucky State University, the land grant college for Black people in Kentucky, established in 1887.

3. EDUCATIONAL OPPORTUNITY

1. In 2021, still grappling with COVID-19 and vaccines, applications were down to just over three thousand.

2. The Office of Institutional Research and Assessment at Berea, like all colleges, does not yet know if and how COVID-19 impacted these and other data.

3. Berry, an American historian, was director of Berea's Appalachian Center and then dean of faculty before assuming this role.

4. Berea calculates that the total cost of educating one of its students is about $43,000, of which $12,000 accounts for room, board, and fees.

5. Students resubmit FAFSA annually. If a student's family contribution changes—either increases or decreases—the formula might change, but the student has time to plan with the help of Berea's Office of Financial Aid.

6. Make two circles with your thumbs and forefingers. The shape on the left looks like a lowercase *b*. The shape on the right looks like a lowercase *d*. Bread on the left; drink on the right.

7. International students and some domestic students stayed on campus, separated, and living alone in several dormitories under strict rules.

4. LIBERAL ARTS

1. Joshua Guthman, *Strangers Below: Primitive Baptists and American Culture* (Chapel Hill: University of North Carolina Press, 2015).

2. "A Note on Methodology: 4-Year Colleges and Universities," *Washington Monthly*, August 28, 2022, https://washingtonmonthly.com/2022/08/28/a-note-on-methodology-4-year-colleges-and-universities-13/.

5. INCLUSIVE CHRISTIAN VALUES

1. Brutus Clay, the elder brother of Cassius Clay, lived in Paris. He was a Presbyterian and a slaveholder and "leased out" about twenty slaves a year to local farmers and small businesses.

2. Acts 17:26.

3. "How Politics Spoiled the Church: The Evangelical Movement Spent 40 Years at War with Secular America. Now It's at War with Itself," *Atlantic*, June 2022.

4. Helen Tworkov, "Agent of Change: An Interview with bell hooks," *Tricycle*, Fall 1992.

6. LEARNING THROUGH LABOR AND SERVICE

1. The largest college farms tend to be at universities with land grant histories, such as Cornell, the University of Wisconsin, and the University of California at Davis.

2. This is the same Theodore Weld who, as a student at Lane in 1834, hosted the famous debates on abolition and then left disgusted by the reaction of the board.

3. E. Henry Fairchild was president of Berea (1869–1889) at the same time that one of his brothers, George, was president of Kansas State Agricultural College and another, James, was president of Oberlin College

4. In 2021, more than 50 percent of students graduated with no debt.

5. When the Arts and Crafts movement came to the United States, many places, including Boston, Minneapolis, New York, and Hull House in Chicago, became active centers.

6. Women's Exchanges still exist in scores of cities and towns around the United States.

7. THE KINSHIP OF ALL PEOPLE

1. Berea does not include international students in those percentages.

2. Carter Woodson was the second Black American after W. E. B. Du Bois to receive a PhD from Harvard.

3. Woodson chose to celebrate Black History Week in February to commemorate the birthdays of both Abraham Lincoln and Frederick Douglass. It remains that way.

4. His brother Robert was president of the University of Chicago.

5. China, India, South Korea, and Saudi Arabia send the most students to the United States.

6. Once, Berea made an error on financial need, said Richard Cahill, director of Berea's Center for International Education, and a Middle Eastern student not only went home every vacation but also brought a fancy car to campus.

7. The Concert Choir, the Bluegrass Ensemble, and the Country Dancers require auditions.

8. A DEMOCRATIC COMMUNITY

1. The civil rights movement in Kentucky Oral History Project at the Kentucky Historical Society. Interview conducted by Betsy Brinson.

2. Dwayne Mack, a professor of history at Berea, interviewed alumni and staff people who participated, and those interviews are in the Hutchins Library's Special Collections at Berea.

3. Dr. Martin Luther King Jr., "'How Long? Not Long' Speech Text," Voices of Democracy, n.d. https://voicesofdemocracy.umd.edu/dr-martin-luther-king-jr-long-not-long-speech-text/.

4. The Institute on Democracy and Higher Education's data shows that 80 percent of all college and university students attend in-state institutions and that their voter participation is higher than that of students who attend institutions out of state; thus, it recommends that colleges focus more attention on voter turn-out of out-of-state students. This information might help Berea further refine its future activities.

9. A SUPPORTIVE AND SUSTAINABLE CAMPUS

1. In 2021, the US Forestry Department reported that approximately 473,000 families, individuals, estates, and other nonindustrial entities owned more than 10 million acres of Kentucky's 12 million acres of woodlands, which represents 48 percent of the state. Patterson considers a forest a forest if it is somewhere between twenty and forty acres.

2. Not being from Appalachia, I use *hollow* instead of *holler*, although *holler* is far more musical and descriptive.

3. Mason accepted a position at the US Department of Agriculture.

4. *Outdoor Magazine* declared Berea's Pinnacles the best hike in Kentucky.

5. The Global Alliance for Buildings and Construction reports that 28 percent of global emissions come from heating and lighting buildings.

6. A business major whose last labor assignment was in the Human Resources Office at the college, he now works for a private company that provides benefit counseling to individuals.

10. SERVING APPALACHIA AND ITS PEOPLE

1. Buckhorn in southeastern Kentucky was first built as an orphanage for impoverished mountain children, centered on a large Presbyterian Church built from logs and now listed on the National Register of Historic Places.

2. One miner always pasted a note in her hard hat for her two sons in case anything happened to her. It said, "I love you, but I am not doing this because of you. I am doing it for myself."

3. In one of its surveys, CEP reported 53 percent of all women miners had been propositioned and 17 percent reported physical attacks, including attempted rapes.

4. See websites for Kentuckians for the Commonwealth and Earth Justice, as well as *Science*, September 10, 2007.

5. Kentucky Department of Energy and Environment.

6. Building on what was already happening on the local level, the US Department of the Interior is currently analyzing the potential of making eastern Kentucky a national heritage site.

7. Since EPG is not in the department of business, it is not certified by the Association to Advance Collegiate Schools of Business. Likewise, Berea has never received grants from the Kauffman Foundation for Entrepreneurship, as EPG is a fully endowed program at Berea.

BIBLIOGRAPHY

Adams, Ellen E. "From Kentucky to Chazy: Anna Ernberg and the Berea Fireside Industries." Alice T. Miner Museum, March 4, 2016. http://minermuseum .blogspot.com/2016/03/from-kentucky-to-chazy-anna-ernberg-and.html.

Adelman, Garry, and Mary Bays Woodside. "A House Divided: Civil War Kentucky." American Battlefield Trust. Accessed December 9, 2019. https://www.battle fields.org/learn/articles/house-divided-civil-war-kentucky.

Alvic, Philis. *Weavers of the Southern Highlands.* Lexington: University Press of Kentucky, 2009.

American Battlefield Trust. "Kentucky in the Civil War." September 20, 2019.

Anderson, James D. *The Education of Blacks in the South, 1860–1935.* Chapel Hill: University of North Carolina Press, 1988.

ASHE (Association for the Advancement of Sustainability in Higher Education). "2019 AASHE Annual Report." 2019. https://express.adobe.com/page /OCbBtNqCvGvoo/.

Beazley, Ernie. "Champion of the Woman Miner." *New York Times,* October 7, 1979. https://www.nytimes.com/1979/10/07/archives/champion-of-the-woman -miner.html.

Berry, Wendell. "Conserving Forest Communities." 2013. http://tipiglen.co.uk /berryfc.html.

———. *Think Little: Essays.* Vol. 1. Berkeley, CA: Counterpoint, 2019.

Blanchard, Mary Warner. *Oscar Wilde's America: Counterculture in the Gilded Age.* New Haven, CT: Yale University Press, 1998.

Boles, John B. *Religion in Antebellum Kentucky.* Lexington: University Press of Kentucky, 1976.

Boris, Eileen. *Art and Labor: Ruskin, Morris, and the Craftsman Ideal in America.* Philadelphia: Temple University Press, 1986.

Boyce, Robert Piper. *Building a College: An Architectural History of Berea College.* Berea, KY: Berea College Printing, 2006.

Brice, Ernst. "The Protestants and Baptism, Be They Reformed, Lutheran or Evangelical Baptist." Protestant Museum. Accessed January 28, 2022. https://musee protestant.org/en/notice/the-protestants-and-baptism-be-they-reformed -lutheran-or-evangelical-baptist/.

Brooks, David. "The Dissenters Trying to Save Evangelicalism from Itself." *New York Times,* February 4, 2022. https://www.nytimes.com/2022/02/04/opinion /evangelicalism-division-renewal.html.

Broomfield, Sarah Stopenhagen. "Weaving Social Change: Berea College Fireside Industries and Reform in Appalachia." Textile Society of America, October 2006. https://digitalcommons.unl.edu/tsaconf.

Brown, James S. *Beech Creek: A Study of a Kentucky Mountain Neighborhood.* Berea, KY: Berea College Press, 1988.

Burnside, Jacqueline Grisby. *Berea and Madison County.* Charleston, SC: Arcadia Publishing, 2007.

———. "Berea's History." Early History of Black Berea (1860–1900): Before Kentucky's Day Law in 1904. Berea College, 2001. https://community.berea.edu/earlyblackberea/bereahistory.html.

———. "Philanthropists and Politicians: A Sociological Profile of Berea College, 1855–1908." PhD diss., Yale University, 1988.

Campus Compact. "Presidents' Declaration on the Civic Responsibility of Higher Education." May 23, 2009. https://compact.org/resources/presidents-declaration-on-the-civic-responsibility-of-higher-education.

Canady, Andrew McNeill. *Willis Duke Weatherford: Race, Religion, and Reform in the American South.* Lexington: University Press of Kentucky, 2016.

Caradonna, Jeremy L. *Sustainability: A History.* New York: Oxford University Press, 2014.

Carlson, Scott, Jay Antle, and Nilda Mesa. "What Sustainability Looks like Now." *The Evolving Campus* podcast, December 9, 2021. https://podcasts.apple.com/us/podcast/what-sustainability-looks-like-now/id1598199058?i=1000544491785.

Catte, Elizabeth. *What You Are Getting Wrong About Appalachia.* Cleveland, OH: Belt Publishing, 2018.

Caudill, Harry M. *Night Comes to the Cumberlands: A Biography of a Depressed Area.* Boston: Little, Brown, 1963. Reprint, Ashland, KY: Jesse Stuart Foundation, 2001.

Chambers, Cassie. *Hill Women: Finding Family and a Way Forward in the Appalachian Mountains.* New York: Ballantine Books, 2020.

Cline, Austin. "What's the Difference between Religion vs Spirituality?" Learn Religions, June 25, 2019. https://www.learnreligions.com/religion-vs-spirituality-whats-the-difference-250713.

College Stats. "Why Men Are Falling Behind in Higher Ed." Accessed February 17, 2022. https://collegestats.org/2013/05/why-men-are-falling-behind-in-higher-ed/.

Cooper, Anna Julia. *A Voice from the South.* Xenia, OH: Aldine Printing House, 1892. Digital facsimile from original at William L. Clements Library, University of Michigan. Available online at Google Books.

Cowen, Scott. *Winnebagos on Wednesdays: How Visionary Leadership Can Transform Higher Education.* Princeton, NJ: Princeton University Press, 2018.

Daniels, Ronald J. "Universities Are Shunning Their Responsibility to Democracy." *Atlantic*, October 3, 2021. https://www.theatlantic.com/ideas/archive/2021/10/universities-cant-dodge-civics/620261/.

Dorgan, Howard. *Giving Glory to God in Appalachia: Worship Practices of Six Baptist Subdenominations.* Knoxville: University of Tennessee Press, 1987.

Dupuy, Mary P. "Opportunity School Comes of Age." *Mountain Life & Work,* 1945.

Eller, Ronald D. *Uneven Ground: Appalachia since 1945.* Lexington: University Press of Kentucky, 2013.

Entrepreneurship in American Higher Education: A Report from the Kauffman Panel on Entrepreneurship Curriculum in Higher Education. Kansas City, MO: Kauffman Foundation, 2006.

Executive Office of the President. "Increasing College Opportunity for Low-Income Students: Promising Models and a Call to Action." Washington, DC, 2014. http://www.oecd.org/edu/.

Fairchild, E. H. *Berea College, Kentucky: An Interesting History; Approved by the Prudential Committee, 1875.* Cincinnati, OH: Elm Street Printing Company, 1875. Digital facsimile from UK Library Special Collections Research Center, University of Kentucky. https://exploreuk.uky.edu/catalog/xt7hdr2p6114 #page/4/mode/1up.

Fallin, Wilson, Jr. *The African American Church in Birmingham, Alabama, 1815–1963: A Shelter in the Storm.* London: Routledge, 1997.

Fee, John Gregg. *Autobiography of John G. Fee: 1816–1901, Berea, Kentucky.* Chicago: National Christian Association, 1891. Digital facsimile available from Documenting the American South, Academic Affairs Library, University of North Carolina–Chapel Hill. https://docsouth.unc.edu/fpn/fee/fee.html.

"Feminist Group Assails Coal Industry." *New York Times,* May 12, 1978. https://www.nytimes.com/1978/05/12/archives/feminist-group-assails-coal-industry-time-for-support-new-jobs.html.

Foner, Eric. *Reconstruction: America's Unfinished Revolution, 1863–1877.* New York: Harper & Row, 1988.

Foner, Eric, and Joshua Brown. *Forever Free: The Story of Emancipation and Reconstruction.* New York: Knopf, 2005.

Fox, John, Jr. *The Little Shepherd of Kingdom Come.* New York: Avon Books, 1973.

Frost, William G. "Matilda Hamilton Fee, 1824–1895." 1895. Digital facsimile of pamphlet available from Berea Book Collection, Berea College. https://berea .access.preservica.com/uncategorized/digitalFile_1a664c90-ad6a-4312-b557 -ef205e74cd7d/.

Harlow, Luke E. "The Religion of Proslavery Unionism: Kentucky Whites on the Eve of Civil War." *Kentucky Historical Society* 110, no. 3/4 (2012): 265–91. https://www.jstor.org/stable/23388053.

Henry, Stuart C. "The Lane Rebels: A Twentieth Century Look." *Presbyterian Historical Society* 49, no. 1 (1971): 1–14.

Hine, Darlene Clark. "Carter G. Woodson, White Philanthropy and Negro Historiography." *History Teacher* 19, no. 3 (1986): 405–25. https://doi.org/10.2307 /493381.

Hood, Abby Lee. "Women Miners Work to Record a More Complete History of 1980s Labor Strikes." *Daily Yonder*, September 6, 2021. https://dailyyonder.com/women-miners-history-of-1980s-labor-strikes/2021/09/06/.

hooks, bell. *All About Love: New Visions*. World Literature Today. New York: HarperCollins, 2001.

Hopkinson, Deborah, and Don Tate. *Carter Reads the Newspaper*. Atlanta: Peachtree Publishing, 2019.

Horwitz, Ilana M. "I Followed the Lives of 3,290 Teenagers: This Is What I Learned about Religion and Education." *New York Times*, March 15, 2022.

House, Silas, and Chris Green, eds. *Hills and Hollers: An Appalachian Reader*. Berea, KY: Berea College Printing, 2018.

Howard, Victor B. *Black Liberation in Kentucky: Emancipation and Freedom, 1862–1884*. Lexington: University Press of Kentucky, 2015.

———. *The Evangelical War against Slavery and Caste: The Life and Times of John G. Fee*. Selinsgrove, PA: Susquehanna University Press, 1996.

Humphrey, Richard Alan. "Biblical Patterns for Mountain Living." *Appalachian Heritage* 8, no. 3 (1980): 69–78. https://doi.org/10.1353/APH.1980.0002.

Hutchins, Francis S. *Berea College: The Telescope and the Spade*. New York: Newcomen Society, 1963.

Jones, Loyal. *Reshaping the Image of Appalachia*. Berea, KY: Berea College Appalachian Center, 1986.

Keim, Brandon. "Blowing the Top Off Mountaintop Mining." *WIRED*, September 7, 2007. https://www.wired.com/2007/09/mountaintop-mining/.

Kentucky River Authority. "An Introduction to the History of the Kentucky River as a Transportation Route." 2010. https://finance.ky.gov/kentucky-river-authority/Documents/2_Intro_Ky_River_Trans_Route.pdf.

Leonhardt, David. "The Growing College Graduation Gap." *New York Times*, March 25, 2018. https://www.nytimes.com/2018/03/25/opinion/college-graduation-gap.html.

Levy, Harold O., and Peg Tyre. "How to Level the College Playing Field." *New York Times*, April 7, 2018. https://www.nytimes.com/2018/04/07/opinion/sunday/harold-levy-college.html?smid=url-share.

Lexington History Museum. "E. Belle Mitchell Jackson." Lex History, June 4, 2021.

Logan, Rayford W. "Carter G. Woodson: Mirror and Molder of His Time, 1875–1950." *Journal of Negro History* 58, no. 1 (1973): 1–17. https://doi.org/10.2307/2717153.

Lucas, Marion B. *A History of Blacks in Kentucky: From Slavery to Segregation, 1760–1891*. Frankfort: University Press of Kentucky, Kentucky Historical Society, 2003.

Lull, Herbert Galen. *The Manual Labor Movement in the United States*. University Studies. Seattle: Bulletin of the University of Washington, 1914.

Mack, Dwayne. "Ain't Gonna Let Nobody Turn Me Around: Berea College's Participation in the Selma to Montgomery March." *Ohio Valley History* 5, no. 3 (2005): 43–62. https://muse.jhu.edu/article/572954#info_wrap.

Maimon, Alan. *Twilight in Hazard: An Appalachian Reckoning.* Brooklyn: Melville House, 2021.

Masten, April F. *Art Work: Women Artists and Democracy in Mid-Nineteenth-Century New York.* Philadelphia: University of Pennsylvania Press, 2008.

McWhorter, John. "What Should We Do About Systemic Racism?" *New York Times,* September 10, 2021. https://www.nytimes.com/2021/09/10/opinion /systemic-racism-education.html.

Mockrin, Miranda H., Rebecca L. Lilja, Emily Weidner, Susan M. Stein, and Mary A. Carr. "Private Forests, Housing Growth, and America's Water Supply: A Report from the Forests on the Edge and Forests to Faucets Projects." General Technical Report 327. Fort Collins, CO: Rocky Mountain Research Station, Forest Service, US Department of Agriculture, 2014. https://doi.org/10.2737 /RMRS-GTR-327.

Morgan, Charles T. *The Fruit of This Tree: The Story of a Great American College and Its Contribution to the Education of a Changing World.* Berea, KY: Berea College Press, 1946.

Muir, John. "The American Forests." *Atlantic Monthly* 80, no. 478 (September 1897): 145–57. https://cdn.theatlantic.com/media/archives/1897/08/80-478 /131953245.pdf.

Mullainathan, Sendhil, and Eldar Shafir. *Scarcity: Why Having Too Little Means So Much.* New York: Henry Holt, 2013.

Nelson, Paul David. "Experiment in Interracial Education at Berea College, 1858–1908." *Journal of Negro History* 59, no. 1 (1974): 13–27. https://doi.org/10.2307/2717137.

Nettles, Mary "Beth." "Women's History Month." US Department of Labor blog, March 22, 2022. https://blog.dol.gov/tag/womens-history-month.

Newman, Rich, and Stanley Harrold. Review of *The Abolitionists and the South, 1831–1861* by Rich Newman. *Arkansas Historical Quarterly* 55, no. 3 (1996): 329. https://doi.org/10.2307/40030986.

Obas, Kenley H. "The History of Historically Black Colleges and Universities and Their Association with Whites." *International Journal of Education and Human Developments* 4, no. 1 (2018).

Oswalt, Sonja N., and W. Brad Smith. "U.S. Forest Resource Facts and Historical Trends." 2012. https://www.srs.fs.usda.gov/products/marketing/cards/fs-1035 .pdf.

Packer, George. "Can Civics Save America?" *Atlantic,* May 2021. https://www .theatlantic.com/ideas/archive/2021/05/civics-education-1619-crt/618894/.

Pappano, Laura. "At Christian Colleges, a Collision of Gay Rights and Traditional Values." *New York Times,* June 5, 2018. https://www.nytimes.com/2018

/06/05/education/learning/christian-colleges-lgbtq-social-justice.html
?searchResultPosition=1.

Patrick, Andrew Parker. "Inner Bluegrass Agriculture: An Agroecological Perspective, 1850–1880." *7° Convegno Nazionale Di Viticoltura, Piacenza, 9–11 Luglio 2018*, 2012.

Patterson, Clint. *A Century of Forestry at Berea College*. Berea, KY: Berea College, 2018.

Peck, Amelia, and Carol Irish. *Candace Wheeler: The Art and Enterprise of American Design, 1875–1900*. New York: Metropolitan Museum of Art, 2001.

Peck, Elisabeth Sinclair, and Emily Ann Smith. *Berea's First 125 Years, 1855–1980*. Lexington: University Press of Kentucky, 1982.

Plymouth Church. "Henry Ward Beecher." Accessed November 9, 2018. http://www.plymouthchurch.org/beecher.

Quarles, Benjamin.. "Sources of Abolitionist Income." *Journal of American History* 32, no. 1 (1945): 63. https://doi.org/10.2307/1892887.

Rainforest Alliance. "What Is Sustainable Forestry?" July 28, 2016. https://www.rainforest-alliance.org/insights/what-is-sustainable-forestry/.

Recruiting and Retaining Students in a Challenging Market. Washington, DC: Chronicle of Higher Education, 2021.

Ribuffo, Leo P. "Jesus Christ as Business Statesman: Bruce Barton and the Selling of Corporate Capitalism." *American Quarterly* 33, no. 2 (1981): 206–31. https://doi.org/10.2307/2712316.

Rice, Connie Park, and Marie Tedesco. *Women of the Mountain South: Identity, Work, and Activism*. Athens: Ohio University Press, 2015.

Richardson, Harold Edward. *Cassius Marcellus Clay: Firebrand of Freedom*. Lexington: University Press of Kentucky, 2015.

Rogers, John Almanza Rowley. *Birth of Berea College: A Story of Providence*. Philadelphia: Henry T. Coates, 1903. Digital facsimile available from Internet Archive. https://archive.org/details/birthofbereacolloroge/page/n5/mode/2up.

Rutkow, Eric. *American Canopy: Trees, Forests, and the Making of a Nation*. New York: Scribner, 2012.

Saul, Stephanie. "As Flow of Foreign Students Wanes, U.S. Universities Feel the Sting." *New York Times*, January 2, 2018. https://www.nytimes.com/2018/01/02/us/international-enrollment-drop.html.

Sayre, Laura, and Sean Clark, eds. *Fields of Learning: The Student Farm Movement in North America*. Lexington: University Press of Kentucky, 2011.

Schweiger, Beth Barton. "The Literate South: Reading before Emancipation." *Journal of the Civil War Era* 3, no. 3 (2013): 331–59.

Sears, Richard. "John G. Fee, Camp Nelson, and Kentucky Blacks, 1864–1865." *Kentucky Historical Society* 85, no. 1 (1987): 29–45.

———. *Kentucky Abolitionists in the Midst of Slavery (1854–1864): Exiles for Freedom.* Lewiston, NY: Edwin Mellen Press, 1993.

Sears, Richard D. *Camp Nelson, Kentucky: A Civil War History.* Lexington: University Press of Kentucky, 2002.

———. *A Utopian Experiment in Kentucky: Integration and Social Equality at Berea, 1866–1904.* Westport, CT: Greenwood Press, 1996.

Second Nature. "The Presidents' Climate Leadership Commitments." 2007. https://secondnature.org/signatory-handbook/the-commitments/.

Sinha, Manisha. *The Slave's Cause: A History of Abolition.* New Haven, CT: Yale University Press, 2016.

Smiley, David L. "Cassius M. Clay and John G. Fee: A Study in Southern Anti-Slavery Thought." *Journal of Negro History* 42, no. 3 (1957): 201–13. https://doi.org/10.2307/2715937.

Smith, Christi Michelle. *Reparation and Reconciliation: The Rise and Fall of Integrated Higher Education.* Chapel Hill: University of North Carolina Press, 2016.

Smith, Miranda. "Danforth Chapel at Berea College." Clio: Your Guide to History. July 25, 2019. https://theclio.com/entry/83906.

Stephenson, Martha. "History of Education in Kentucky." *Kentucky State Historical Society* 15, no. 44 (1917): 67–79.

Stottman, M. Jay, and Lori C. Stahlgren. "Uncovering the Lives of Kentucky's Enslaved People." Kentucky Archaeological Survey, 2017. https://transportation.ky.gov/Archaeology/Documents/Uncovering%20the%20Lives%20of%20Kentucky%27s%20Enslaved%20People.pdf.

Strange, Jason G. *Shelter from the Machine: Homesteaders in the Age of Capitalism.* Champaign: University of Illinois Press, 2020.

Svrluga, Susan. "Liberal Arts Education: Waste of Money or Practical Investment? Study's Conclusions Might Surprise You." *Washington Post,* January 14, 2020. https://www.washingtonpost.com/local/education/liberal-arts-education-waste-of-money-or-practical-investment-studys-conclusions-might-surprise-you/2020/01/13/5a197b14-3649-11ea-bb7b-265f4554af6d_story.html.

Taylor, Amy Murrell. *Embattled Freedom: Journeys through the Civil War's Slave Refugee Camps.* Chapel Hill: University of North Carolina Press, 2018.

Thomas, William R., Jeffrey W. Stringer, Terrance E. Conners, Deborah B. Hill, and Thomas G. Barnes. "Kentucky Forest Fact Sheet." UK Cooperative Extension Service, 2007.

Thompson, Derek. "Colleges Have a Guy Problem." *Atlantic,* September 14, 2021. https://www.theatlantic.com/ideas/archive/2021/09/young-men-college-decline-gender-gap-higher-education/620066/.

Tierney, John. "Career-Oriented Education vs. the Liberal Arts." *Atlantic,* November 20, 2013. https://www.theatlantic.com/education/archive/2013/11/career-oriented-education-em-vs-em-the-liberal-arts/281640/.

Water Power & Dam Construction. "Hydro for Higher Education." March 24, 2022. https://www.waterpowermagazine.com/features/featurehydro-for-higher -education-9575007/.

Weld, Theodore D. *First Annual Report of the Society for Promoting Manual Labor in Literary Institutions*. New York: S. W. Benedict, 1833.

Wiewel, Wim. "The Case for Liberal Arts Education in a Time of Crisis." *New Republic*, May 27, 2020. https://newrepublic.com/article/157845/case-liberal -arts-college-coronavirus-crisis.

Wilson, Charles Reagan. "Religion and the US South." *Southern Spaces*, March 16, 2004. https://doi.org/10.18737/M74C77.

Wilson, Dreck Spurlock, ed. *African American Architects: A Biographical Dictionary, 1865–1945*. New York: Routledge, 2004.

Wilson, Shannon H. *Berea College: An Illustrated History*. Lexington: University Press of Kentucky, 2006.

Woodson, Carter G. *The Education of the Negro Prior to 1861: A History of the Education of the Colored People of the United States from the Beginning of Slavery to the Civil War*. Chicago: Association for the Study of Negro Life and History, 1915. Reprint, Whitefish, MT: Kessinger Publishing, 1919.

Wyatt-Brown, Bertram. "American Abolitionism and Religion." Divining America, TeacherServe, National Humanities Center. Accessed February 24, 2023. http://nationalhumanitiescenter.org/tserve/nineteen/nkeyinfo/amabrel.htm.

Yarnell, Susan L. "The Southern Appalachians: A History of the Landscape." General Technical Report SRS-18. Asheville, NC: Southern Research Station, Forest Service, US Department of Agriculture, 1998. https://www.srs.fs.usda.gov /pubs/gtr/gtr_srs018.pdf.

Zinn, Howard. *People's History of the United States: 1492 to Present*. New York: HarperCollins, 1980.

Zipf, Catherine W. *Professional Pursuits: Women and the American Arts and Crafts Movement*. Knoxville: University of Tennessee Press, 2007.

INDEX

Page numbers in italics refer to photographs.

Howard, Oliver O., 26
Howard Hall, 26
Howard Hall Memorial Park, 26
Howard University, 26, 33
Hull House (Chicago), 153, 169n5
Humphrey, Hubert, 102–3
Hutchins, Francis S., 11, 67, 101–2, 115–16, 147
Hutchins, Robert, 170n4 (ch. 7)
Hutchins, William J., 6–7, 9, 101
Hutchins Library, 5, 170n2
hydropower, 135–36

International Development Placement Association (IDPA), 102–3
international study, 41, 45–46, 106

Jackson, Belle Mitchell, 23, 26
Jackson, Jordan, 26
Jackson Energy Cooperative, 136
Jackson State University, 42
Johnson, Lyndon, 117, 142
Jones, Preston, 153
Jones, Robert, 17
Julett (enslaved woman), 16

Kansas State Agricultural College, 128, 169n3 (ch. 6)
Kelley, David, 102
Kennedy, Jackie, 114
Kennedy, John F., 102–3
Kentuckians for the Commonwealth, 91
Kentucky Department of Agriculture, 123
Kentucky Federation of Women's Clubs, 153
Kentucky Historical Society Oral History Project, 170n1 (ch. 8)
Kentucky State University, 101, 168n10
King, Davey, 155
King, Martin Luther, Jr., 11, 115, 116–17
Kinloch, David, 135
Kitenda, Samson, 44, 65
Klanderud, Jessica, 95, 100

Labor Program, 7–8, 31, 42, 67, 79–82, 155, 159
Lakes, Chris, 11, 48–49
Lakes, Greg, 148
Lane Theological Seminary, 13, 14, 20, 79, 167n1 (ch. 2), 169n2 (ch. 6)
Lawson, LaDarious (Samez), 47–48
Leis, Ben, 61, 64, 71, 73
Lewis, John, 5, 114, 116
liberal arts education, 52, 60, 100, 157
Lilly, Eli, 68
Lincoln, Abraham, 22, 170n3 (ch. 7)
Lincoln Institute, 29–30
Liuzzo, Viola, 117
Log House Craft Gallery, 83, 85
Long Seals, Ashley, 45, 74–76

Mack, Dwayne, 116, 170n2
March on Selma, 5, 114–17
Margaret Cargill Natural Sciences and Health Building, 132
Marks, Jonathan, 52
Martin, Hannah, 55
Mary Reynolds Babcock Foundation, 92
Mason, Silas C., 128, 129, 130–31, 171n3 (ch. 9)
Matilda Hamilton Fee Hydroelectric Station, 136
Mbewe, Gertrude, 52, 54
McDaniel, Hunter, 86–88
mental health services, 160
Merton, Thomas, 105
Middletown, Laquita, 64
Miles, Taylor, 77, 89
Mitchell, Belle, 23, 26
Mitchell, Sharyn, 130, 141
Morehouse College, 68
Morton, J. Sterling, 129
Mountain Day, *109*, 110
Move-In Day, 43
Ms. Foundation for Women, 142
Muir, John, 129
Mullainathan, Sendhil, 49

Society for Promoting Manual Labor in Literary Institutions, 79
Sodexo, 123
Spelman College, 33
sports, 33, 37, 108–9
Stephenson, Jane, 140
Stephenson, John, 91, 103–5, 140, 148
Stewart, William B., 79
Stone, May, 153
Stover, Aaron, 74
Strange, Jason, 18, 44
Strayed, Cheryl, 54
student chaplains, 69–71, 119
Student Craft program, 5, 9, 82–86, 132–33, 140
Student Government Association (SGA), 113, 115, 118, 119–20, 122
Student Nonviolent Coordinating Committee, 114
Students for Democratic Action (SDA), 102
Suffolk Punch horses, 125, 126, *127*, 128
sustainability, 123–37

Tandy, Vertner Woodson, 29
Tapia, Kevin Moreno, 108–9
Tarbell, Ida, 84
Taylor, Breonna, 117
Taylor, W. C., 28
Test of English as a Foreign Language (TOEFL), 106
Think Globally, It's Friday (TGIF), 106–7
Thompson, Teri, 141, 155
Tibetans, 103–5
Tillery, Tristan, 53, 119
Timby, Ben, 122
TOEFL, 106
Tolstoy, Leo, 71–72
tourism, 145–46
Toynbee Hall (London), 153
Trail Towns, 145, 146
Truman, Harry, 118

Truth Talks, 97–98
Tufts University Institute on Democracy and Higher Education, 118
Tuskegee Institute, 29, 99
Tworkov, Helen, 76

Underground Railroad Bicycle Route, 145
United Mine Workers, 143
University of California at Davis, 169n1 (ch. 6)
University of Chicago, 170n4 (ch. 7)
University of Iowa, 68
University of Kentucky, 89
University of Wisconsin, 169n1 (ch. 6)
Upward Bound, 110–11
US Department of Agriculture, 171n3 (ch. 9)
US Department of Education, 40
US Department of Energy, 135
US Department of Labor, 143, 144
US Department of the Interior, 171n6 (ch. 10)
US Forestry Department, 170n1 (ch. 9)

Vanderbilt, George, 129
Vanderfleet, Marilyn, 143
Van der Ryn, Sim, 134
Vassar University, 33
volunteer work, 121–22
voter registration, 118–19
Voting Rights Act (1965), 117

Wallace, George, 114, 116
War on Poverty, 140
Washington, Booker T., 99
Watson Fellowships, 46, 88, 111
Weatherford, Willis, Jr., 11, 68
Weckman, Judith, 65
Weld, Theodore, 79, 167n1 (ch. 2), 169n2 (ch. 6)
Wesleyan University, 167n3 (ch. 1)
Wheeler, Candace, 83–84

White, Spicy, 130
Wilkinson, Howard, 105
William and Mary University, 167n3 (ch. 1)
Willis D. Weatherford, Jr. Campus Christian Center. *See* Campus Christian Center
Wilson, Woodrow, 113–14
Wisconsin Idea, 139

Women's Exchange, 83, 169n6
Woodson, Carter G., 99, 169n2 (ch. 7), 170n3 (ch. 7)
Woodward, Matthew, 66
Work College Consortium, 4
Wright, Carol, 136
Wright, LeSette, 65

Zechar, Tongtu, 61–62, 73, 113